Advance F

Next! is a must read for anyone looking to "get off the wheel" and truly own their career. Scott Moore tells his personal story in a way that everyone can relate. Scott proves that success doesn't come from simply working harder, but instead by taking chances in yourself and working smarter. I wish that I had a copy of this book when I started in the financial services industry over forty years ago!

~ Tom Burns , former Chief Distribution Officer
Allianz Life Insurance Company North America

Scott Moore has accomplished a goal that many have dreamed of, but few have successfully obtained. Without hesitation and with the resources he had, Scott combined great effort and persistence along with a strong commitment to develop a thriving company. He created a formula through arduous planning that would take him from his present situation to the future he envisioned and dreamed about. His plan is presented in a such a straight-forward and clearly defined way, that anyone desiring to build a multi-advisor financial practice has the formula. With a good strategy, along with commitment, persistence, sacrifice and hard work, you too can accomplish your goals. In *Next!*, Scott gives you the formula. If you desire to be successful in your business, I highly recommend that you read *Next!*. It will take you to the *Next* level!

~ William H. Cain, CEO, Financial Independence Group

In *Next!* you'll learn Scott Moore's incredible system for recruiting qualified associates and his sales success, including how to train others to ask questions, listen effectively, address objections before they are ever asked, and how to close sales. These techniques work. I used them to become an award-winning, top-producing sales manager, first in the financial services sector, and then in real estate. Everyone told me real estate was risky. However, using the skills I learned from Scott, I went forward into real estate with confidence and immediately built a six-figure income which I have maintained for years. Scott taught me how to set a big vision and create a successful career in not one, but two industries. Read this book, apply what you learn, and your future will be very bright.
~*David Mills, Real Estate Broker Associate, Lakewood Ranch, Florida*

"In *Next!* Scott Moore shares his story of grit and determination to overcome the adversity of starting a small business. Combining sound business processes and sound decision-making Scott establishes a blueprint that can enable others to achieve their American dream." ~*Matthew D. Miller, M.S., LPC, NCC*

"I have known Scott for thirty-five years. His perseverance, dedication and ethics while raising a strong family and creating a successful business helping others is a tribute to his personal character. This book is a rare gem outlining unique procedures to establish trust with your clients and build a stellar reputation for your business in the community. I am excited that Scott is now sharing his *Next* adventure of coaching and mentoring current and future entrepreneurs. A quick read guaranteed to increase your personal success." ~*John T. Trotter, J.D., Retired Millionaire Publisher*

NEXT!

A Blueprint to a Million-Dollar Income in the Financial Services Industry

M. Scott Moore

THOMAS NOBLE
BOOKS

Wilmington, DE

THOMAS NOBLE BOOKS

Author Contact: ScottMooreConsulting.com
Thomas Noble Books
Wilmington, DE
www.thomasnoblebooks.com

ISBN: 978-1-945586-20-0
First Printing: 2019
Printed in USA
Editing by Suzanne Gochenour
Cover Design by Sarah Barrie
Internal Design by Balaji Selvadurai

This publication is designed to provide accurate and authoritative information regarding the subject matter covered. It is sold with the understanding that the author is not engaged in rendering professional services. If legal, accounting, medical, psychological, or any other expert assistance is required, the services of a competent professional person should be sought. Client names have been changed to protect identities.

Dedicated to Carla, my amazing and incredibly supportive wife of thirty-eight years and to my wonderful children, Chris, Brian, Kyle, Jonathan, and Michelle. Thank you all for supporting me in my dream. I love you all and am incredibly proud of each one of you.

TABLE OF CONTENTS

FOREWORD

I've been in the financial services industry for over forty years and can honestly say that Scott Moore is one of the best advisors I've ever encountered. Scott has a unique ability to create business processes that succeed. I've observed him spending hours considering the best way to do each thing in his business, hone those ideas, and then, teach the processes to others so well that they can replicate his success.

Now that Scott's written, *Next!*, financial advisors all around the country will benefit from Scott's discoveries. If you want more success and financial reward in your financial services career, pay close attention to everything you'll discover in this book, both the practical ideas as well as the important mindset information. There is gold in this book for advisors with strong ethics, willingness to try new things, and a strong work ethic. Scott models all these positive traits and more.

As you read, you'll be inspired. Scott could be a poster child of a rags to riches story. When I met him, he could barely pay his bills, even though he was working many hours and doing all he could to succeed. Over the years, I've watched him succeed beyond his wildest expectations using the tools and mindset he shares in this book. Whether you are a new or seasoned financial advisor, the information in this book will help you achieve your goals with integrity.

If you have a burning desire to succeed in the financial services industry, this book will help you. I strongly recommend *Next!*

and Scott's outstanding mentoring programs. Get a notebook and start making lists of ideas as you read. Follow Scott's example and implement those ideas with commitment and enthusiasm. Your success awaits.

Gary Reed
President and Founder
Reed Financial Group

INTRODUCTION

Are you ready for your next opportunity? Do you work in the financial services industry, either for a large corporation or in a solo independent practice? Are you a burned-out Corporate America professional? Maybe you have an entrepreneurial drive and would like to become a successful financial advisor with your own agency or firm. Would you be interested to know that it is possible for you to have more—more money, more satisfaction, and more opportunities to serve your clients?

If you were to hang around with me for a day, you'd frequently hear me saying "Next!" Whenever a problem or challenge arises, I use that term to remind myself to move on and focus on a solution.

There is a problem in our industry. Many good advisors are often working long hours without enough compensation and little hope for the future. Just eleven years ago, I was sleeping in my car at rest stops in between out-of-state appointments, too broke to afford a motel room. At the same time, I was winning awards for outstanding production as a financial advisor. I was stuck and felt like a rat on a wheel in a cage. No matter how hard I worked, I could not earn enough to get ahead.

I don't know about you, but awards and trophies won't pay my bills. A few years later, after nineteen years as a high-producing, award-winning advisor for one of the largest companies in the United States, I loudly stated "Next!" I left my captive position and opened an independent wealth management firm. This created a million-dollar income for myself and improved my quality of life. And with honesty, strong ethics, and integrity, I was able to provide some good people with outstanding incomes of their own.

This book tells you how I did it, and how you might be able to replicate my success.

Enjoy it and dream big. Your Next! future awaits.

CHAPTER 1

GETTING OFF THE WHEEL

Ted looked at me with pride in his eyes as he put down his coffee cup. He shared that after thirty-six years working for one of the largest financial services firms in the United States, his annual gross income (before expenses) was one hundred seventy-five thousand dollars. In that environment, he was a high-producing success. I understood his feelings because I spent nineteen years with the same organization and worked extremely hard to earn a similar income.

As our conversation continued, I told him that my income increased to five hundred seventy-five thousand dollars in my first year as an independent advisor. It continued to grow as I added additional advisors to my company. I revealed that I'd reached the million-dollar mark on my personal tax return in just five years and continued growing annually. That additional income changed the future of my family, all of it earned ethically and honestly.

However, Ted started to look over his shoulder as he listened. "Scott, I feel like I'm committing treason just by talking to you, but I thank you for opening my eyes," he confessed as we left the restaurant. I felt sad for Ted. He was trapped like a rat on a wheel in a cage and thought he was unable to do anything to improve his income and quality of life. He did not believe that he could have more success or that there were other options available to him.

If you are currently working for an insurance or financial services company or are in a one-person independent agency, what you read in this book is going to open your eyes. You're going to learn why I left my position as an award-winning mutual fund broker and life insurance agent at one of the largest companies in the United States after nineteen years. I'll describe in detail how I built a multi-advisor financial services firm and grew my income to the million-dollar level in five years. Moore's Wealth Management was voted the #1 Financial Planning Firm in North Georgia in 2016, 2017, and 2018. The company has no debt and a business valuation between seven and ten million dollars.

It's difficult to find precise numbers on how many financial services professionals are working in the United States today. The best estimate is that there are eighty-six thousand independent advisors and forty-one thousand captive advisors working for large companies. On the insurance side, there are an estimated five hundred forty-eight thousand independent life insurance agents and one hundred ninety thousand captive agents. If you are one of those nearly nine hundred thousand professionals working hard every day for your clients and your family, or one of the millions of individuals looking for a way to start or transition into the financial services world, this book is for you. I'm not simply going to tell you to work harder, sell more, or maximize your advertising dollars, although those topics will certainly be covered. Nor will I suggest sleazy, unethical tactics to get clients to invest in things they don't need.

Instead, in this book, you'll read an honest account of how I took a risk that changed my life and business forever. I'm going to tell you the story of how I built a multi-million-dollar agency in a small southern town where I had no contacts or history. Today, that business is widely respected as an ethical, stable firm where people feel comfortable investing their life savings. You will read about my successes and challenges, as well as what I have learned along the way.

Why Am I Sharing This Information?

I love this industry and the honor of helping people safeguard and grow their life's savings. I've been blessed to work with some incredible mentors and wonderful clients over the years. Like many of you, I've worked alongside other advisors busting their backs to provide outstanding service with high integrity.

Unfortunately, I've also seen some who take shortcuts with the truth. It's a dirty little secret in our industry that many financial advisors are desperate for money. They have no savings or investments for their future. I didn't follow my own advice either when I was working for a large company and had very little set aside for a retirement plan. You can imagine how guilty I felt advising people to save and invest their money for the future while I was scraping by month to month. Things got so bad that I declared personal bankruptcy in 1999, stemming from mounting medical bills of my dying mother in addition to the normal financial challenges of raising five children. I moved to a new state with more opportunities to start over.

That shame made me feel like an imposter for a long time, even though I was one of the highest producers in my company.

Today, my life is entirely different. I live in a beautiful eight thousand square foot home on a lake, in the Blue Ridge mountains. I take two to three months of vacation each year, and my personal income varies between six hundred thousand and a million dollars annually while personally writing no production or business. These changes did not occur because I won the lottery or cheated my clients. My life changed when I left my position at one of the biggest financial services companies in the nation and started an independent agency.

There is a better way to grow and succeed in the financial services industry. If you are an ethical and hardworking financial advisor, you deserve to grow your career as far as you want to take it. If you are hungry for more than what you have today, the information in this book can help you.

An Unlikely Success

Before delving into methods, let me tell you about my background. I didn't grow up with a silver spoon in my mouth or around people with great wealth who could open doors for me.

Raised in Gulfport, Mississippi, I am the youngest of four children. My father died in 1970 when I was just seven years old. My mother never remarried and worked extremely hard to take care of us until she passed away in 1998. Our family always struggled with money. I began selling newspapers when I was eight years old, giving my earnings to my mother. From then on, I always had a job, doing whatever I could to help my mother keep us together. Some of my high school and college jobs included working at small motels as a porter, the midnight shift at Krystal Hamburgers and at a Naval retirement home, doing dishes in the kitchen. In fact, one of my friends recently reminded me of the work he and I did in the school cafeteria to pay for my meals, throughout junior high.

At age nineteen, I married my wife, Carla (age eighteen) in 1981. You'll hear a lot about Carla in this book. She's my best friend and has been with me through many struggles and triumphs. We got married right out of high school and were parents of five children by the time I was thirty.

I was a good student, but there were no funds for me to attend a major university. So, I went to a business college in Gulfport and graduated in 1982 with an associate degree in electronics.

From 1982 to 1991, I worked in the computer industry, as a field engineer for Telex and Data General Corporation, moving seven times in nine years. Then I became a technical sales support representative for an IBM value-added reseller in New Orleans. We moved a lot as I got promoted, from Mississippi to Louisiana, then to Kansas, and later back in Louisiana to New Orleans. We were blessed with five children. Carla stayed home to raise them, and I did everything I could to earn enough to support our growing family. It was not easy. I was working twelve to fifteen hours per day, on call almost every weekend to cover maintenance issues at large accounts. Carla was raising our four sons and one daughter without me.

In 1987, we went to Florida on a family vacation. Instead of enjoying the beach that weekend, I locked myself in the hotel room and read Harvey Mackay's book *Swim with the Sharks Without Being Eaten Alive.* That book taught me about creating a need and filling it. I figured out that my employer in New Orleans needed a new position, a Vice President of Sales Support, and convinced him to let me fill this position. This move gave me a 25% pay raise (to fifty thousand dollars per year), which helped a lot, but it still wasn't enough to cover my family's needs.

During this time, Carla became adept at cooking delicious meals on two dollars a day and wearing three-dollar dresses. Our kids were growing like weeds and always needed new clothes and larger shoes. Money was so tight in the Moore household that we were rolling coins and cashing in Coke bottles to buy groceries. My current career just wasn't enough to cover our needs, no matter how many hours I worked or how carefully Carla managed our household budget.

In 1990, I started a part-time career in finance working twenty to twenty-five hours per week, while keeping up with my demanding day job in computers. I worried about money so much that I wanted to learn more about how it worked: how to earn it, save it, and invest it.

I discovered a talent for working in this area and was able to replace my computer engineering salary within nine months. It was risky working entirely on a commission basis, but I went full time in 1991. I was a life insurance agent and mutual fund broker for almost nineteen years. In that time, I won many awards, was selected to serve on the Field Cabinet, which less than one half of the top one percent of financial services representatives in the country ever achieve.

At the same time, I struggled with serious health challenges. At twenty-seven I was diagnosed with an aggressive form of rheumatoid arthritis, the same disease that led to my father's early demise when he was fifty-three. There were times I was in such bad shape I could not get out of bed in the morning and had to crawl to the bathroom. Frankly, I was embarrassed, discouraged and apprehensive, but fought through it daily. I loved my family dearly. What would happen to them if I could no longer work or died young as my father did?

I hid my medical issues at work and strove to earn as much as I could while I was still able to work. I did everything I could to change my financial situation and became known as a crazy workaholic who drove all over the southeast to find clients. Up until 2008, I worked eighteen to twenty hours most days. That's when I often slept in my car. On one trip funds were so scarce, I removed the backseat of the car searching for coins to purchase enough gas to get home. Carla managed everything at home and was always supportive, but the pressure on us was intense. Something had to change.

In late 2008, my good friend Paul Roberts set up an interview for me with Gary Reed. He was the president of a small field marketing organization (FMO) and well-known throughout the independent financial advisor industry. He even sat on the prestigious Advisory

Board of one of the largest insurance companies in the world, Allianz. When Gary called to schedule the interview, he asked if I could meet him for breakfast the next morning at 8:00 a.m. I was so excited that I agreed, even though I was in Mobile, AL at the time. That was six hours away from Northeast Atlanta where Gary was, and I still had three more appointments that evening. By the time I finished, it was after 11:00 p.m.

Instead of trying to get some rest after an eighteen-hour day, I drove all night to get back to my home in Atlanta. I arrived there at 6:00 a.m., showered and changed into my best suit and tie, and made it to the early breakfast. I had not slept in over twenty-six hours, but Gary never knew that until a few years later. Folks, opportunity only knocks once or twice in life for most of us. You have to be ready to do whatever it takes to seize it when it shows up at your door. Because I made that interview, my life changed forever. I risked it all and left the captive environment to start my independent financial services firm. In 2009, I almost quadrupled my gross income. By the year 2013, my personal income was a million dollars. The business and my income have grown every year since. It's been an incredible blessing.

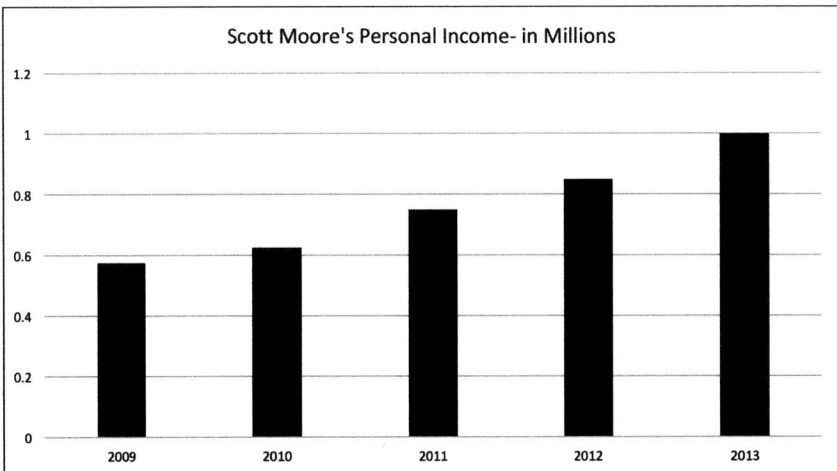

Scott Moore's Personal Income- in Millions

Year	Income
2009	0.58
2010	0.63
2011	0.76
2012	0.85
2013	1.0

I had no option but to succeed. Thankfully, I did, and now enjoy a life and career that's everything I ever wanted and more. I've also been able to bring some of my children into the agency and provide them with a career that makes their lives much more rewarding than mine ever was at their ages.

So, What's Next for You?

If you want more, have a strong work ethic, a high degree of integrity, and a willingness to learn, you can achieve a greater level of success than you have today. Read this book with an open mind. Examine the facts and then decide if becoming an independent financial advisor with a multi-advisor firm is right for you.

I'm going to tell you the truth, this path is a lot of work, especially in the beginning. I'm going to share all my experiences in these pages. You'll discover what I learned, where I made errors and how I corrected them. You'll learn both the personal and professional skills required to grow your own independent agency. This solution is not for everyone. However, if you have what it takes, you put in the effort, and you follow these instructions, you can and will change your life.

Thank you for investing time to read and consider these ideas. Let's begin now. Your future is waiting. Next!…

CHAPTER 2

SEVEN YEARS TO $50 MILLION OF NEW ASSETS PER YEAR

Do you remember *Dragnet*? Whether you recall the black and white television show or the movie with Dan Ackroyd, you probably remember Joe Friday's phrase, "Just the facts." Our industry depends on facts and numbers, percentages of growth, and progress over time.

Let's examine the facts of my first seven years as the owner of a multi-advisor financial services firm. I'm now in year eleven with an incredible lifestyle. First, you'll observe that the firm grew in a step-by-step process. We started small, worked extremely hard, and evolved over the years.

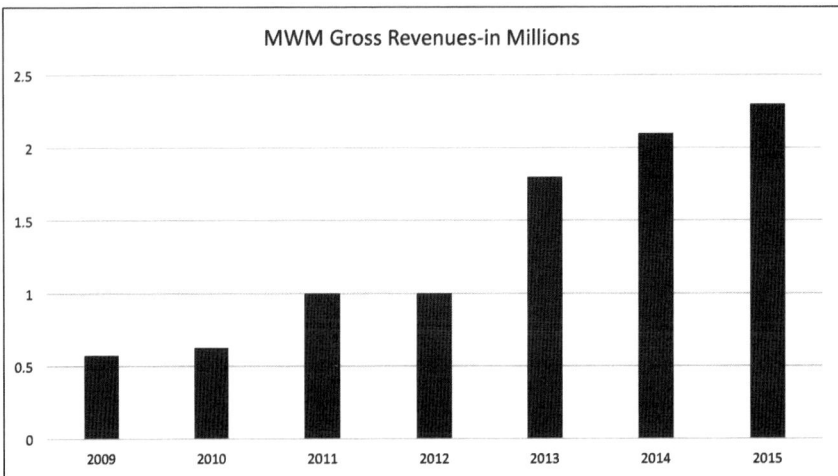

MWM Gross Revenues-in Millions

Year	Revenue (Millions)
2009	~0.58
2010	~0.63
2011	~1.0
2012	~1.0
2013	~1.8
2014	~2.1
2015	~2.3

Next, the numbers reflect steady growth each year. I remember some of my colleagues were skeptical when I first started to grow. They thought my initial success was a fluke, a lucky break, or good timing. However, we were able to maintain this every year, despite the ups and downs of the market. This continued increase in clients and income is the result of hard work, careful planning, and specific processes.

I am not a financial wizard or the smartest guy you've ever met. My gift is an ability to create processes and procedures, hone them over time, and then teach them so that others can be successful. Everything you'll read in the rest of this book I based on the specific processes I used and taught to my associate advisors. This information helped me to experience more success and financial reward than I ever dreamed possible when I was a struggling advisor working seventy to eighty hours a week just to pay my bills. My average annual gross income (before expenses) back then was one hundred fifty thousand dollars. My best year at that large company was one hundred eighty-nine thousand dollars.

That's a decent income for a captive advisor, but when you deduct all office expenses, overhead, and taxes from this amount, the remainder is much less. I wanted more for my family. You probably do too. Here are the facts and numbers of my first seven years as an independent advisor.

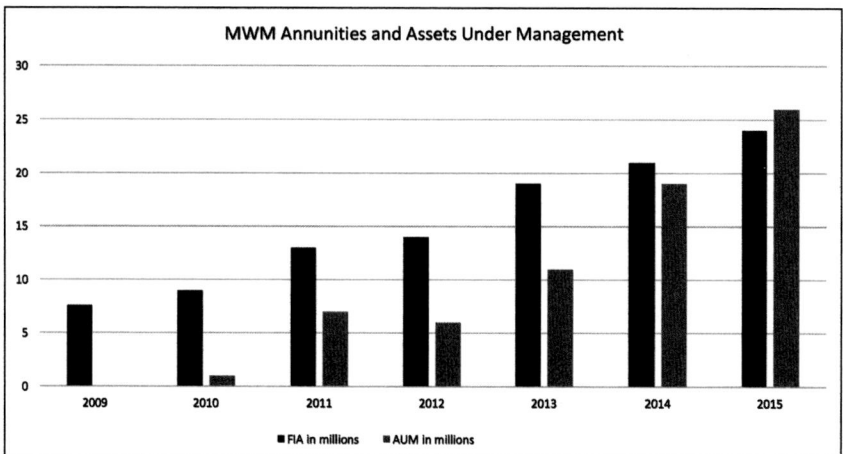

MWM Annunities and Assets Under Management

FIA=Fixed Index Annuity

AUM=Assets Under Management

2009: 1st Year of Moore's Wealth Management

- $7.6M FIA (personally written new business)
- One office with three family members staffing it—myself, son Chris, and wife Carla
- Securities License (Brokerage Series 6, 26, and 63) on Hold
- 50% Growth over 2008's annuity production as a captive advisor, and 400% Growth on gross income, as an independent advisor.

2010: 2nd Year

- $10M TOTAL NEW BUSINESS (personally written new business)
- 40% Growth over 2009 in production
- Hired office manager
- Passed S65 Exam: Fiduciary Advisor Exam
- Conducted 25 seminars—10% referrals

2011: 3rd Year

- $20M TOTAL NEW BUSINESS (personally written new business)
- 100% Growth in production over 2010
- Began to train Chris as an associate advisor
- Hired son Brian as case preparation specialist
- Opened 2nd office
- 40 seminars—20% referrals
- Family Practice Financial Coaching: Family members underwent counseling to learn how to work productively together. This training was absolutely essential to our success. Three days of on-site training and follow-up cost $15,000 but paid great dividends.

2012: 4th Year

- $20M TOTAL NEW BUSINESS (personally written new business)
- Maintained Volume and Increased Profit
- Doubled main office space
- Added Mark Peterson as an associate advisor
- 22 seminars—50% referral business versus 20% in 2011
- Continued to write all new business myself

2013: 5th Year

- $30M TOTAL NEW BUSINESS (personally involved in all new business)
- 50% Production Growth over 2012
- Began training Brian as an associate advisor
- Chris and Mark began to write some new business with my support
- Formed a Client Advisory Council
- Added 20 college courses to the seminar schedule
- All marketing/mailing expenses paid by our Field Marketing Organization (FMO)
- $50K main office expansion to 3,000 sq. ft.—240 people attended the Open House
- Secured corporate/penthouse apartment within walking distance of office to avoid two-hour daily commute.
- Segmenting cases/Multiple advisors: Chris, Mark, Brian—All S65 licensed
- Hired son Kyle as a Case Support Specialist

2014: 6th Year

- $40M TOTAL NEW BUSINESS (personally written new business)
- 30% Production Growth over 2013

- Added Bill Johnson as a coach for high net worth clients (Approx. $1,000/mo. fee. Well worth it!)
- Added additional college courses to our seminar schedule
- Increased branding with local events and wrote newspaper column articles
- All marketing/mailing expenscs paid by FMO
- Increased Volume for all advisors: Chris, Mark, and Brian wrote 60% of new business while I wrote 40%

2015: 7th Year
- $50M TOTAL NEW BUSINESS
- 25% Production Growth over 2014
- Transitioned 400 client accounts to new securities custodian
- Hosted our largest client appreciation event with more than 300 attendees
- All marketing/mailing expenses paid by FMO
- Associate advisors wrote 75% of new business, and I wrote 25%

Today Moore's Wealth Management is valued between seven to ten million dollars. We manage approximately 300 million dollars of assets. The agency has a well-designed succession plan that will transfer ownership to my fellow advisors when I am ready to exit the business. We continue to grow our client base and personal revenues every year.

These are the facts of my journey. If you like these numbers and want to learn how I achieved them, continue reading.

M. Scott Moore

CHAPTER 3

MY MULTI-ADVISOR INDEPENDENT AGENCY MODEL

You've read how I worked for nineteen years in a captive environment for a well-known financial services company. At one point, I was close to burning out and considered quitting the financial services industry to return to engineering. Then, at a national conference, I met a woman who changed my life. She worked in the same corporation as I did and we both lived in Atlanta. We were not in the same hierarchy, so she was not obligated to help, but she did. She was a very successful sales director and took me under her wing and mentored me for several years. Because of her leadership and my willingness to be coachable, she changed my family's life.

One of the most important things I learned from her was the importance of ensuring that I made enough money to take care of my family first. I was astounded that many of my colleagues had little savings and struggled financially. She showed me how to avoid some critical pitfalls and increase my income. To do that, I had to work contrary to the company's business model of only recruiting and building and spend more time on client acquisition. At the time, this was a risky and revolutionary choice, but I had a big family and needed to do whatever it took to earn enough to care for them.

After a few years, my friend Paul Roberts, who had an independent agency, showed me how I could offer a broader array of products and services to my clients if I became independent. Because of being captive at my current agency, I was limited to only the products they provided. He showed me that if I worked independently, I could offer my clients more investment and insurance options to better meet their needs, effectively cutting out the middleman and making a more substantial income for myself.

It was a risk, but after my research, consultation with my wife and my mentor, I decided to open my own independent financial services agency. In one year, my gross income rose from one hundred fifty thousand (earned as a captive agent) to five hundred seventy-five thousand dollars as an independent advisor. I maintained the same work ethic, but now with a much greater income opportunity, it changed my life and the future of my family. Within seven years, Moore's Wealth Management had fifty million dollars in new annual assets coming in each year, offices in two locations, and I had a team of associate advisors and a full administrative staff. Today, we have three locations, maintain over two hundred million dollars of FIA business and approximately one hundred million dollars in active AUM investment business.

I share this information to show you what can be possible for an advisor brave enough to work independently and willing to follow a proven model of growth. It is not easy, but it is indeed possible for those who are willing to put in the time and effort required. So many advisors, upon discovering a better system, as I did in 2009, will put in less work. And because I mentioned before that opportunity usually only knocks once or twice in life, I decided to keep the strong work ethic I had already developed. I could have worked less and still earned a better income, but that was not my goal. While I still had fairly decent health and some youth on my side, I gave it all I had, which is why I am where I am today.

Step one is to understand the business model I employed.

Becoming Independent

Simply put, when you are an independent advisor, you can offer clients insurance and investment vehicles from many companies instead of just the ones represented or owned by the company with whom you are captive. There is no hierarchy above you, taking part of your profits. You have more flexibility for your clients and more money coming to you. You also better your quality of life and can do more to help your clients.

In my opinion, this is the absolute best way to fulfill your fiduciary responsibility to clients. You are no longer confined to a specific group of financial vehicles. You can develop portfolios for your clients with products from an independent variety of companies, precisely tailored to meet the goals of your clients. That is not always possible when a company dictates what you can and cannot offer. You no longer have to only choose from "what's in the wagon."

The standard arrangement for a captive advisor is a small office for the advisor and an administrative support person. They work in a particular community or territory. In some cases, several advisors work out of the same office. Money is often tight, so the office furnishings do not inspire respect. Rather than being known as a fantastic financial advisor, you are the local guy or gal who works for XYZ insurance or investments. The parent company has the brand and the name. Captive advisors are usually seen as interchangeable and replaceable.

These environments are not usually where investors with a high net worth feel comfortable investing their life savings. I have no judgments against investors with a modest amount of money to invest. However, if you are motivated to increase your income significantly, you will need more clients with a higher net worth.

To move from a captive environment to an independent advisor, you'll need to research and make business agreements with various investment and insurance companies as well as FMO's and compliance agencies. You'll also need to secure licenses for securities, a good accountant, required business licenses, and ensure that everything you do creates a climate of trust. As long as you comply carefully with all laws and regulations, you'll truly be your own boss, able to do things your way.

Becoming a Multi-Advisor Agency

When I left the captive environment, the last thing I wanted to do was recruitment. I'd spent years, as a captive agent, recruiting potential advisors, and thousands of hours training them. Those hours were on top of all my work with client acquisition and service, often occurring on weekends and evenings. I'd pour everything I had into my recruits, only to have many of them quit or cause problems. The industry standard is that if you recruit 100 people, an average of 20 will stay with you (the old 80-20 rule). But only two individuals of those 20 (the 2% rule) will eventually achieve some measure of success.

Then, there is the burden of responsibility for the people you recruit. If one of your recruits does something shady or unethical, you are tainted and responsible for their behavior even if you were unaware of their actions. Despite my best efforts and supervision, I had a problem with two or three associate advisors at one time and had to pay over two-hundred fifty thousand dollars in chargeback roll ups as settlement for the associates' misbehaviors. It was extremely difficult to get ahead financially on a personal basis when this type of liability was constantly present.

At the time I opened my agency, I had no plans to build a multi-advisor agency. However, as my business grew, I could not keep up with client demand. I brought on my sons, and later, a middle-aged friend, to work as advisors with me.

Recruiting and training advisors is the most critical part of your success for owners of a firm like mine. It's more challenging than finding the right investment vehicles, compliance, and sales. Recruitment, training, and ongoing supervision of advisors can fail for several reasons.

First, many successful financial advisors do not have written processes. They are great at sales, have a loose structure in mind, and can bring on many clients. However, it can be challenging for them to transfer those systems to others. My engineering background led me to develop written processes for almost everything in my office. Before I brought in an associate advisor, I'd already documented and tested the procedures. That helped me greatly.

Many advisors don't like an observer during sales situations. They may find it unsettling to have a trainee watching their every move during client appointments, either because those advisors lack high-level skills or because they like to bend the rules a bit. In our industry, roughly 20% of advisors serve 80% of the clients, so many advisors are not personally successful enough to train others.

Then, there is a lack of training skills. The skills required as a financial services advisor are very sales-oriented. You must be able to listen intently, talk with people, convey trust, and serve them at a high level so that they remain your client over the long term. Those skills do not often overlap with the skills required to recruit, train, and mentor advisors for months or even years until they are ready to work on their own.

Finally, some solo producer independent agencies do not have the financial reserves to pay an attractive base salary to a potential associate advisor while the recruits are learning and not producing income. Even re-structuring your office to include another desk and meeting space for an additional person can be difficult if you have not grown the agency income sufficiently.

I don't tell you these things to discourage you in any way. Instead, I want you to understand that growing a successful multi-advisor agency takes time and effort but can give you marvelous rewards, both financially and personally. It's a journey with many steps. In later chapters, you'll discover how you can complete that journey successfully, whether you are currently in a captive environment or own a small independent agency.

CHAPTER 4

RISKS AND BENEFITS OF THE MULTI-ADVISOR MODEL

When I worked in a captive environment, I won a lot of awards. I had shirts, jackets, trophies, and plaques galore. One prize was so big I had to hire a truck to get it to my office. At that time my children were young, so Carla and I would need a sitter when we attended the awards banquets. Our next-door neighbors in Louisiana, a kind older couple, were our favorite sitters for these events. Mr. Jay, who was retired from a forty-year career at Western Auto, was a bit of a father figure to me.

I'll never forget the night when we came home all excited from another awards ceremony where my company honored me. I was happy and proud. Mr. Jay turned to me and said, "Scott, your company clothes you and gives you lots of stuff to hang on the wall. But are you making any money?" I didn't know what to say.

It would be several years later that I started to look at my income seriously. I was a top producer and celebrated within the company. On the other hand, I worked insane hours, including evenings and weekends, and my income was not moving up much. I had little time to see my family, and we struggled to make my income cover our expenses. All my hard work wasn't getting me much except applause and trophies. Literally, I needed something I could take to the bank!

You've heard the saying "The definition of insanity is doing the same thing over and over again while expecting different results." Under that definition, my career path was pretty insane. If you are working in a captive environment, you may be experiencing the same questions I struggled with back then.

We're financial advisors. Our training is to examine risks and benefits. Let's apply that lens to working for a large financial services corporation, or to the question of keeping your solo independent agency to see if changing makes sense.

Familiarity is one of the most significant benefits of maintaining your current situation. You know your colleagues, supervisors, and products. The captive environment provides the advantage of working for a recognizable brand. The familiar routine, advertising methods, and periodic meetings pump you up. You may even have a mentor in the organization. You feel loyal, and create a stable association record on your resume. Staying put can be a safe and wise choice for many advisors.

However, there are definite risks, especially if you want to offer your clients the very best options and increase your personal standard of living. The first risk is a firm limit on your income. I have friends who remain at my former company. In the eleven years since I've been an independent advisor, they are still making about the same income, roughly one hundred fifty thousand dollars annually. With the assistance of a well-trained and dedicated office team, my income is six hundred thousand to one million dollars each year, for doing the same type of work. I worked hard then, and I continue to work hard, but the rewards are so much greater. The good news is that you can also earn these rewards by following the guidelines set forth in this book.

Because I have other advisors working with me in my independent firm, we can serve more clients, offer outstanding client experiences, and have the security of an agency that now has approximately three hundred million dollars in total client assets.

Working in a captive environment, you may only offer your clients the products and services your company owns or represents. Every investment, annuity, policy, or plan you write includes a commission or fee to your company, and sometimes to the people who recruited you. There are more fingers in the financial pie. Also, it is hard to claim you are meeting your fiduciary responsibility to give your clients the very best options when your choices are limited to only the products and services your parent company offers.

As a captive advisor, I was always hoping things would change. I expected to have more options for my clients, hoped that the matrix pay grid would change, and wished the people I recruited would succeed. I could hope those things would improve, but I had no control over any of them. Stuck on my wheel, running faster and faster, I was getting nowhere. I experienced burnout and disillusionment. My body protested the long hours in the car and the overloaded weeks. Any hope for a positive change shrank each year.

However, I didn't feel I could share these concerns with anyone. My family made many sacrifices so I could succeed. I can remember coming home from the office and Carla would have our five children lined up at the door to greet me. My dinner would be waiting in a bowl on the bathroom counter so I could hastily eat while showering and shaving before my evening appointments. Many times, when I would come out of the bedroom about to leave the house, Carla would have all the kids sing in unison, "Go, Daddy, Go! Go, Daddy, Go!" I'd rush out the door right after that to find a note taped on the steering wheel in my car that stated: "You're A STUD!" While I felt great about all of this, I greatly loathed having to leave my family six nights per week, after working a full six days, just to make a decent living. Once I drove off, I often wouldn't make it home until after midnight. I missed bedtimes, ball games, and many church and school performances. Everyone in our family sacrificed so I could win. How could I tell them that all those sacrifices were making little to no difference?

This problem was not specific to me. My recruits were working long hours and making similar sacrifices. They were embarrassed that they couldn't provide for their families as they wished. Some would confide that their spouses were losing faith in them and complained about shouldering all the responsibilities at home. Their marriages were crumbling. Others shared problems with children, who felt they were unloved and ignored because one parent was always away.

Admitting to personal difficulties can be a dangerous practice in our industry. We are trained to be confident, tireless advisors who are always strong. No one wants to appear weak or disloyal for questioning the status quo. We see everyone else apparently managing home and work effortlessly and assume there is something wrong with us for struggling. Eventually, something is going to break. It may be your health, marriage, or the relationships with your children, or all of the above. You know where your vulnerabilities are and the risks you take to give your all, year after year.

Even the mentoring relationship is risky in some settings. If your mentor is helping you only as a means to earn an override on your sales, how honest can they be about your struggles?

On the other hand, if you are mentoring others in a captive organization, you are also at risk. I know a woman who is a superstar in her traditional financial organization. She's built a high income over years of extreme effort. She received promises of rewards for her work and excellent mentoring, but nothing materialized. However, one of her recruits, a young man, decided to start his agency within that firm. Management allowed him to cherry-pick her most profitable clients. By making her mentee a success, her income and client list were damaged and drastically reduced, an outcome entirely out of her control, but too familiar. The company knew she would rebuild her business since she did it once already.

In Corporate America, companies often give their loyalty to profits rather than people. Your immediate supervisor could receive termination papers tomorrow or one of your mentees given perks you deserve. Compensation structures are subject to unexpected changes. Additionally, new laws currently on the books will impact our industry. At this point, we don't know how each large firm will decide to comply with these ambiguously worded laws. We are not even sure of the future of those laws, given the changing political landscape. In a time of industry change, trusting a large corporation with your financial destiny may or may not be a risk you are willing to take.

Finally, you risk never knowing what your real potential can be. Staying as you are, you will not have the opportunity to stretch and explore what's possible. Growing the skills in leadership, sales, and entrepreneurship required to have a successful multi-advisor independent agency will offer you new challenges and opportunities. There will be a tremendous learning curve. Success is not instant nor is it guaranteed. It will require hard work and preparation. But putting the time and effort into forming your own agency is an investment in your personal success, instead of the profits of the organization you serve. If you are a person dedicated to personal growth, this can be an exciting pathway. If you feel frightened by the prospect of so much change, this career option may not be a good fit.

You Don't Have to Decide Immediately

Now that you have reviewed some of the benefits and risks of staying as you are in your captive agency position or your small independent agency, you are probably mentally assessing your situation. If you are anything like me, your brain is whirling with ideas and possibilities, fears, and reasons why you should or should not make a change.

I want you to wait to decide on your future. It is too vital for you and your family to be hasty. Instead, I invite you to keep assessing as you read the rest of this book. Pay close attention to upcoming chapters that detail some of the personal skills you need to move into a multi-advisor business model. It is not for everyone.

However, if you have the desire and drive to succeed and grow your financial future and your ability to serve more clients more profoundly, following this path can be exciting and extremely rewarding. I'm not trying to sell you or convince you to do something you don't want to do. Instead, I'm showing you an alternative future that can possibly be brighter than the one you have now. Read on and wait to decide until you learn more.

CHAPTER 5

MYTHS THAT MAY KEEP YOU BROKE

If you work for a large company, you may have flirted with the idea of becoming an independent advisor but felt it would be impossible. I understand because I thought that way for nineteen years. Many times, we fear change because we don't have a complete picture or all the facts.

In my opinion, these beliefs are myths. However, don't take my word for it. Read the facts, and then you can decide if any of these ideas are strong enough to keep you in your current situation.

Let's take a look at the common beliefs that trap good advisors, to see if they are accurate.

1. "I can't afford to open my own firm." I've heard people say that you need fifty to a hundred thousand dollars saved up to open your financial services firm. When I began my business, I didn't have that kind of cash. I had seven mouths to feed at home and very limited capital, well under three thousand dollars.

So, I worked from a home office for the first six months. I installed a separate business line, carved out an area where I could have privacy, and worked every referral I could find, meeting prospects in their homes. Because I did not immediately open a physical office, I was able to keep my initial costs contained. In the first six months, I saved between fifteen to twenty thousand dollars, which was enough to secure a lease on an office and purchase the necessary furnishings.

I was used to doing the bulk of my meetings in prospect and client homes anyway, so not having an office space at the beginning of my business did not pose any problems. Once I opened my office, I used the next six months to transition my in-home meetings to the office, cutting down on windshield time and making my day much more productive.

I was fortunate not to have to pay large staff expenses during my start-up period. My son Chris worked with me on the advisor side for a minimum salary, and my wife Carla handled the telephones, marketing, and administrative tasks.

If you don't have the benefit of family members who can help you, ask everyone you know for a referral to someone who would like to work on a part-time basis answering the phone and greeting visitors. It is imperative that you don't answer your own business telephone. Having a staff person in the office sends a message about the stability of your company. You may recruit a mother to work when her children are in school or find an intern from a local college to assist you on a part-time basis. You'll learn more about the best kinds of people to hire in a later chapter. If you need to hire help, plan a budget of fifteen hundred to two thousand dollars monthly to cover the salary of a part-time assistant.

2. "I can't take any of my current clients with me because of a non-compete clause." Reviewing the details of your current non-compete clause is essential. Most are written to prevent you from doing business with clients within fifty to one hundred miles of the company office. Know the facts of

your particular situation. Actually, non-compete agreements cannot be geographically overreaching, otherwise they are not legally enforceable.

It is essential to understand that many parent organizations consider life insurance policies sacred cows, due to the ongoing residual income from annual premiums. I was very cautious not to interfere with any of my former clients' life insurance policies. There is a bit more leeway on the securities side. Advisors are tasked with doing what is in the best interests of their client's economic future. If a former client came to me and I could offer them a better investment portfolio, that would be attending to the best interests of that client.

I was very cautious about how I exited my former position and communicated with those clients. I sent them a cordial letter saying that I enjoyed working with them and that their current plans should serve them well. I added a line that if they wished to contact me in the future, they could do so. In that way, I was not actively seeking them out, but merely responding to a call they initiated.

When former clients contacted me, I asked them to sign a letter stating that they reached out to me for assistance and should they decide to move forward with me, it was in their best interests. I kept these letters on file. I did encounter some pushback from my former captive brokerage firm, but the letters from the clients were enough to stop any issues from growing.

Because ethics and maintaining a positive reputation is critical in our industry, I was cautious about serving former clients and did not market to them at all. It was gratifying when they reached out to me, based on the positive relationship we'd built earlier. However, I spent most of my time cultivating new clients and suggest that you do as well.

3. "I'll have to wait a long time to get my Series 65 Fiduciary License." Federal and state regulations governing our industry are in flux. Many of you reading this book operate under a broker's or insurance agent's license. Because the rules are changing, I strongly urge you to consider obtaining your Series 65 licensure as a Fiduciary Advisor. Whether this licensing may be a requirement in the future or not, it provides another level of credibility for an independent advisor.

However, it is not necessary to wait for months to test for this license. My recommendation is that you do all your preparation to take the Series 65 exam while you are still in your captive environment. Take the test as soon as you leave so that you can open your independent agency with this valuable licensure. You can use your current license to generate income while you wait, but the quicker you earn your Series 65 license, the better.

4. "People will see me as unstable because of the change." This myth worried me the most. I stewed about this for a long time and even lost sleep over it. My wife, Carla, helped me sort it out. She reminded me that in every client appointment I would tell people that I based their plans on the best information I had at the time and that I'd let them know if anything changed. She said, "Scott, don't you see? You will be able to offer people better investments, so they will be glad to know they have more options. This change is a plus for your clients."

Once I shifted my perspective, I could see Carla was right. I would have many more options as an independent advisor and more ways to help my clients grow and protect their finances. When former clients contacted me after I moved to my independent agency, they were curious and wanted to learn about the new vehicles I could offer them. No one criticized me for making the change. They were incredibly supportive.

However, I had a long history with my former brokerage firm. My resume demonstrated stability. If you have jumped around from agency to agency, I would recommend you wait to open your independent agency until your resume shows stability and trustworthiness. In our profession, those two items are essential.

5. "I can't open an agency because I am a female." In my experience, many women are terrific financial advisors and have no barriers to becoming independent. Women are often perceived as more trustworthy and nurturing than men. Many widows or single women prefer working with a female advisor. Gender is no barrier to working in finance.

However, be aware that to build a multi-advisor agency, you must develop the skills to guide, supervise, and motivate your team. Regardless of your gender, consider reading books or taking courses on business leadership so that when you are ready to hire additional advisors, you are confident in your abilities.

6. "I don't have the stamina or health to weather the demands of opening my own firm." Depending on your situation, this may be true for you, or it may be a myth. If you are currently a successful financial advisor working on a full-time basis, you are already working hard. Our profession is not one with business hours from nine-to-five. You are probably already working evenings, and perhaps weekends. If you can move in and out of your vehicle, see clients in your office or their homes, and do seminars and presentations, you have the strength you need, although you may require some adaptions.

When I was twenty-seven years old, I received a diagnosis of rheumatoid arthritis. My father had it, and it led to his early demise when I was only seven years old. There were times when I was working so hard and for such long hours that I had to crawl on my hands and knees to the bathroom in the morning because I could not walk. Even today, I have to get up at least two hours earlier than most people so I can do the exercises I need to be able to move well throughout my day.

Some people ask me why I don't just give up and go on disability. My desire to help my clients and to provide for my family is stronger than my pain. I don't tell many people about my condition, so I'm not tempted to use it as an excuse. Of course, my family and close friends know, and are not surprised when I need to sit down or make some adjustments to compensate for my medical challenges. I believe people can use problems as excuses or get up and make something happen. And I don't believe in excuses. Next!

In a way, my medical challenges have been a blessing in disguise. Because my father died early, I was extremely motivated to provide for my family as quickly as possible. I did not want them to experience the poverty I faced as a child. My health has also made me think about everything I do to ensure I am using my energy as wisely as possible. Finally, I can understand the challenges and limitations my clients face as they age. Even though I am an engineer by training, I've learned to be empathetic when others are suffering. There are benefits to every situation if you take the time to look for them.

7. "I have the wrong personality for this." When I learned about personality types, I discovered I'm a technical thinker and a Type A personality. That means I am analytical and driven to work hard to get what I want. That's not the kind of disposition you would imagine could become successful in an industry that depends on sales and personal contact. I'm not your typical smooth-talking salesman.

My personality type has become an asset instead of a detriment. I learned that clients respected my thorough preparation and ability to explain the technical aspects of their situation in easy-to-understand terms. My Type A personality helped me work hard and strive always to improve, regardless of the obstacles.

Whatever your personality, you can find ways to use it effectively in this industry. If you are currently a successful financial advisor in a captive environment, your personality should not hinder your success as an independent advisor. Whether you are an introvert, extrovert, technical thinker, or warm nurturer, if you are effective in the captive environment, those same traits and skills will serve you well in an independent setting.

Personal growth and development are crucial to success in any professional endeavor. I am still learning more effective ways to communicate, lead, and connect with people, even after thirty years in this industry. My associate advisors take their professional and personal development seriously, as well. In this industry, individual skills, confidence, and abilities are our most essential tools for success. You can always learn more about yourself and your strengths. Aim for continual growth and improvement, and you'll be on the path to success.

8. "I can't leave my current situation because I have a lot of new referrals." While you are working in your captive environment, certainly you will want to continue to work hard and do everything you can to take care of your current clients. As part of that process, you should be asking for referrals. However, there is no reason that you cannot hold on to those warm leads and use them after you become an independent advisor. That's what I did. Once I decided to leave my captive situation, I held all my new referrals until I became an independent advisor.

When I followed up on those referrals, and one of them would become a client, I would call the original referring individual to thank them and say something like, "Bill, I sure do appreciate you sending Tom and Joanne my way. They are great people and ended up coming on board with some of our services. We're excited to have them as clients. However, a few things have changed since I talked with you, so they've got a couple of new concepts that might sound a little different than what you have. At some point, I'm happy to sit down with you and Sandra and look at those options, when it makes sense for both of you."

A call like that thanks your referral source, avoids any confusion if Tom or Joanne tell them about their plan and it sounds different, and keeps the door open should your former client wish to meet with you in the future.

9. "This sounds easy. I'll resign today." I am being facetious here. I've never heard this myth. However, I do want to impress upon you the vital importance of careful planning. I spent nine months researching before I decided to become an independent advisor and another three months before I left my captive position.

Be wise and invest the time you need to fully understand the opportunities and responsibilities of being an independent advisor, carefully plan your exit strategy and the first year of your new business, save appropriately, and do all you can to get your ducks in a row before you make the change. Preparation is crucial to your success.

CHAPTER 6

BE A DUCK ON THE WATER

Success in our industry starts and ends with who you are as a person. Your personal characteristics are more important than your intelligence, industry knowledge, or office furniture. That doesn't mean you must be perfect. It just means that a high level of personal skill and responsibility are required for clients and prospects to trust that you will take good care of the money they've worked hard to amass.

Opening an independent financial services agency and growing it by adding other advisors will require the best that you can give. Your name is on the door and the letterhead. When I opened Moore's Wealth Management, I was proclaiming that I, personally, would help my clients, not as an agent of a larger company, but as the President and CEO of my own firm. Any problems would be on my shoulders to fix. If our reputation was stellar, it was because I made it that way. If people doubted our firm, it was because they were doubtful about me. If you are currently working in a captive environment, you represent a parent company. When you become an independent advisor, you represent yourself 100%.

As you review the following list of personal skills required for success, assess yourself. You will have natural strengths and areas for improvement. Once you identify any areas where you need to grow, you can begin to build competence and confidence now, before you make the transition to your own agency. Personal growth is a lifelong pursuit. I work on myself continually and you will too if you are committed to your success.

1. **Imagine a duck floating on a calm lake.** It appears to glide with minimal effort, while under the surface, it paddles furiously. Clients should never sense that you are struggling, tired, stressed out, or worried. Even during times when you are running 100 miles per hour, everything on the surface should look calm and peaceful.

Because our industry requires high levels of trust, you must always appear confident and trustworthy. Learn to paddle as fast as you need to under the surface, but present a calm, relaxed, and reliable public image.

I'm not suggesting that you "fake it until you make it" or mislead others. Instead, I'm suggesting you cultivate a strong professional image and use it consistently in public. You will encounter times when your personal life feels like a tornado has hit. Several years ago, while I was still in a captive environment, one of my granddaughters died unexpectedly. It was a terrible and very difficult experience for my son Chris and our entire family. Unfortunately, as much as I wanted to, I could not stop work for many months like some people might think. At that time, I did not have the financial resources to suspend my work. So, after several days to attend to the details and mourn, I had to return to work, even though I was deeply grieving.

Resist the urge to share any struggles, challenges, or worries with clients and prospects. They are not your therapist. Instead, they want someone who can help them. Share your struggles with your minister, or a trusted friend, and maintain a warm, trustworthy, and professional manner with the public. Be careful not to share too many negative feelings or mental struggles with your spouse. He or she is your biggest cheerleader. They need to see you lead with a positive attitude the majority of the time. This helps their belief in you remain strong.

You must learn to stack things in your favor. There are many obstacles in making a transition and opening a new business. Do all you can to control your image and turn everything into a positive so that your clients' perception is that you and your new firm are stable and secure. This skill of managing your public persona will be helpful for the remainder of your career. Glide like a duck, even if it is only above the surface.

2. **Have a clear and concise mental picture of your success and share it.** When I was transitioning to my independent agency, I worked from home for the first six months to keep my expenses to a minimum. However, before I opened my office, I'd already researched the community and the location for my new office. I was able to tell prospects things like this, "I used to be a broker with a division of a multi-national company, but now I am transitioning to becoming an independent advisor with my own office in Gainesville, GA. Are you familiar with the downtown area there? My new office will be right on the square." As I secured office space, I'd talk about the building, which floor we'd be on, and the month that we'd open the office. Always sell a very distinct vision to your clients and follow through.

To sell with confidence, you must have a solid plan and specific details that you can share. Those particulars gave me confidence my business opening was going to happen. And it helped my prospects to know my transition time was short, with a plan and timeline in place. Imagine if I did not have a clear blueprint for my new business. I'd have to say, "Well, I'm moving to a new office and it's going to be around here somewhere, but I don't have a community or specific location in mind yet." How many prospects would be willing to follow me and invest money in a firm that sounds so disorganized and unstable?

Creating a clear and concise mental picture of your new office isn't about visualizing. It's about research, careful planning, and timing. I had my plan ready to go before I left my former employer. That became a selling point, demonstrating my ability to manage details, and projecting an exciting vision to my prospects and clients.

No one wants to invest their money with a business that appears chaotic and unstable. People can smell fear and chaos. You must have a concrete plan and secure pathway to your future before you make your transition away from your current employer.

However, I do not suggest stopping your forward momentum. If you are a detail-oriented person, you could spend the next ten years planning your exit and never get around to making a move. I am not encouraging you to 'fake it until you make it,' but to create a plan and implement it as quickly as possible. I used a six-month window. That timeframe may be useful for you as well.

3. **Accept that your life will be out of balance at times.** As a new entrepreneur, your business will require the bulk of your time, especially during the first few years. Even later, there will be ebbs and flows. Prepare your family and enlist their support. They will have to do things without you for a while. I missed many of my children's school plays, ball games, and other performances. Thankfully, Carla taught our children that I had to work very hard to earn money for our family and that I did so because I loved them. It was a struggle for all of us, but now we are all reaping the benefit of those long hours.

It is vital you tell your loved ones that this period of arduous work will be time limited. No one, even if they love you dearly, can tolerate your absence forever. Let them know that the next months are going to be challenging. Explain why. It may be the opening of your new office, a cash flow problem, or some other issue. Your loved ones will understand if you share the specific problem and your best estimate on how long you will need to solve it. Then make sure to deliver on your promise. Your family will continue to support you if they have confidence that you will do what you say.

During these intense times, put your hobbies and other enjoyments to the side. Spend all your time either working or with your loved ones. This will demonstrate that you are fully committed to them. If your child wants you to play catch and you'd rather read a book, choose time with your child.

Remember that your family can lose trust in you just as your clients may. If they don't see progress, or you are spending less time with them than promised, their belief in you will falter. Integrity at home is just as important as it is with your prospects and clients.

4. **Learn to compartmentalize your life**. Over my many years of recruiting and training new financial advisors, I've seen many who were not able to separate their home and work lives. A problem at home would become so overwhelming that they could no longer serve or attract clients. Or, issues at work would bleed over into their family and create distrust and worry.

By all means, share your success and progress with your family. Let them celebrate with you, even if it is only a picnic of takeout chicken in the park. However, as I mentioned earlier, be careful of sharing too many of your setbacks. Your family needs to believe in your ability to provide for them. Use your good judgment here.

We all tend to want to dump our problems on our cheerleaders. However, too much of that can cause a loss of confidence and thoughts like, "Wow, if he can't handle losing one client, how is he going to make this new business work?" I made it a rule never to come home and dump all my problems on Carla. She already had a tough time wrangling five kids all day long.

Instead, I would turn to an industry mentor or a business coach when I needed help. Those individuals could look at situations logically and help me to move forward to a quick solution. Support and mentoring are essential. Just be sure to get it from those who can help you with industry knowledge and won't worry about their security when you are struggling. Now I am grateful to give back—mentoring others on their way to the next level.

When you have a family struggle, and you will, you must learn to keep home issues at home. During your working hours, focus on your goals and results. Some people suggest taking time off from work to sort out family problems. Doing so can be a problem if you can't solve the issue in a day or two. I've seen many new advisors with great potential leave the industry because they lost momentum over a divorce, family illness, or another personal challenge.

I'm not suggesting that you become a robot or ignore your loved ones. Instead, I'm saying your career needs to be your priority during your working hours. When you can compartmentalize work and family time, you'll be able to give each its proper attention.

5. **Cultivate positive momentum.** When you focus on achieving results and measuring your success, you'll keep moving forward. You will encounter problems and challenges, that is a given. You have a choice. You can allow challenges to stop you and send you backward, or you can use them as ways to improve your plans and processes. If you can train yourself

to see challenges as opportunities to grow, you'll be able to maintain your positive momentum. Finding creative business solutions can be empowering and exciting if you learn to welcome challenges. Over time, you will build confidence and a solid belief that you can always find a solution. Then setbacks won't stop you, but will become a means to improve. Whether you are facing good times or challenges, always respond to others that things are going "unbelievable." That way you are always truthful, as things could be unbelievably good or bad. This prevents disclosing bad news to others and actually helps motivate you to solve problems and move forward with successful solutions.

6. **Select your mentors wisely.** It is important to have mentors who have achieved greater success than you have. Sure, it can be fun to commiserate with your peers, but they rarely help you as quickly as someone more experienced. Half of your colleagues don't know how to solve your problem, and the other half may be glad you are having trouble so that they can outshine you.

I have always worked with mentors and hired business coaches for specific issues when warranted. Their guidance has been invaluable to my growth and success. I look for mentors more successful than I am, yet still active in the business environment so they can supply information pertinent to the current situation. If you have a mentor who has not been working directly with clients for many years, you run the risk of getting outdated information.

Seek out mentoring and coaching in the areas of business or personal development where you need to grow. There are some who can give you everything you need, but they are rare. You may need to work with one mentor on sales for a while and then another on leadership and staff supervision as you grow.

Of course, you must be open-minded to benefit from mentoring. If you are too proud to admit to struggles or refuse to accept your mentor's suggestions, you will not succeed. There is much to learn when you become an independent advisor— marketing, advertising, sales, new products, leadership, staff supervision, and more. It would be impossible to know everything right away. Take advantage of wise mentors, books, and programs on personal and business development, and self-confidence. When you decide to become a lifelong learner, you'll have the attitude required to soak up all the knowledge you can from your mentors and coaches. Now that I am mentoring others, it is very rewarding to watch them grow and succeed.

7. **Pay attention to your relationships.** If you wanted to build a healthy marriage, you wouldn't spend all your time with someone who has multiple divorces. Your friends will contribute to your outlook and attitude, either positively or negatively. You may need to let some of them go from your life. Try to spend your time with people who model positive values that support professionalism and growth. You may love your high school friend who has a drug problem but decide you don't want him around your family or business.

Some people believe that success is earned from nine-to-five, Monday through Friday. I disagree. Your actions away from work are just as important or greater than those you do at the office. I work in a small southern city where everyone knows everyone. Can you imagine what my reputation would be like if I were seen being drunk and disorderly on Saturday night?

Choose friends who can help you have fun and enjoy life without damaging your reputation. I am blessed with some marvelous friends, neighbors, and mentors who make positive contributions to my life. There are positive, upstanding people in every community who enjoy helping others succeed. Align yourself with them.

8. **Build your confidence.** You would not be attracted to this industry if you lacked this quality. It is a prerequisite in any work that requires selling. Do not neglect to build your self-assurance, as it must grow and develop over time. You'll become more confident each time you learn new skills, master challenges, and achieve results. When you increase your personal income to a level you never dreamed possible, your self-esteem soars. When you track your results and see consistent gains from year to year, you will come to believe you are secure in your professional success.

You've heard many times of the importance of setting weekly, monthly, quarterly, and annual goals. These measures of success are even more critical when you are your own boss. Never neglect goal setting and tracking your results. That is the best way to increase your confidence.

9. **Hone your sales and people skills.** I started my career as an engineer, one of those technical guys with an aversion to salespeople. I'd go to a location to do a job and while completing the task, would always spend time building relationships with the people who worked there. I would shudder when people suggested that I go into sales.

However, I learned there is a difference between a salesperson who will say anything to make a sale and one with a high level of understanding about his or her industry and offerings. A professional gains respect for their expertise, knowledge, and communication skills.

One of the most helpful books I've ever read was Dale Carnegie's *How to Win Friends and Influence People.* Everyone should read this book. There is a reason it has been a top sales classic for decades. Learning to listen, communicate with clarity, and form relationships built on trust and integrity is essential.

Do all you can to become a professional salesperson. Know your products thoroughly. If someone asks you a question you can't answer, be honest, say you'll get back to them, and do it. Listen carefully and maintain eye contact. Prepare for all appointments and presentations well in advance. If you are meeting with a couple, ensure that you are respectful to both the husband and wife. Use people's names. Focus on helping them achieve their financial goals instead of making a sale.

These concepts are not new. You've probably heard them before. However, nothing can replace good listening and people skills. When you communicate that you genuinely care about your clients and prospects, know your products, and are willing to work hard on their behalf, you will earn trust. That trust is everything in our profession.

10. **Embrace Next!** Whenever you encounter a problem in your business or life, follow my example and say," Next!." I say this out loud to remind myself that it's time to move on instead of getting stuck in blame, doubt, or uncertainty. It's important to always look forward. When you point yourself into the future, you'll find a way to resolve the challenge positively, instead of falling into debilitating self-pity.

CHAPTER 7

LICENSING, REGISTRATIONS, AND REGULATIONS

Because you are already active in the financial services industry, you may not think that this chapter is significant for you. You may already hold licenses as an insurance agent or perhaps as a broker or advisor. However, once you become an independent advisor, licensing and regulation become much more critical. You are no longer working in an environment where your parent company dictates the types of licenses you require and oversees your marketing efforts. As an independent, you have more options and choices. In this chapter, you'll get an overview of the required licenses and how each comes with particular regulations that must be followed to comply with that licensing board.

Before we begin our discussion of licensing, let me make one important statement. It is up to you to research the requirements your state has in place for financial advisors. I'll be covering general federal regulations in this chapter, as they apply across the board. However, each state has laws regulating our profession. Once you understand the information in this chapter, you'll be able to ask the right questions and determine your state's requirements for independent advisors.

You may assume that gathering as many licenses as possible is a good idea. I thought so too in my early days as an independent advisor. However, I learned some of the requirements for specific licensing conflict with the provisions of other licensing bodies. The more licenses you have, the more regulations, compliance paperwork, and oversight you will have. Based on my experience, I believe it is best to have only those you need to comply with the law and serve your clients' best interests. In that way, you can focus your creativity on finding and serving your clients instead of working with different regulations and regulatory paperwork. Licensing and compliance are essential in our industry, but wisely selecting the right ones will help you minimize hassles and focus on your clients.

Start Here

Your first license should be life and accident/health insurance, as issued by your state. These licenses have different names in each state but allow you to sell fixed and fixed index annuities, and insurance for life, long-term care, and other forms of protection. Most states call this license the Resident Life and Health Insurance License.

Life insurance is a critical product for all clients. Younger investors need this form of insurance to protect their families. Older investors may use life insurance products to accumulate money inside a policy or annuity with the possibility to withdraw it tax-free. There are both fixed and fixed index annuities which can provide growth and asset protection. You can also offer health care supplement policies and long-term care insurance, which can be an important source of asset protection and peace of mind.

If you do not already possess this license, secure this license first, in the state in which your business resides. Once your state licenses you, you can apply to offer insurance in other states, under a Non-Resident Life-Health Insurance License. I have clients in several states. Each time I get a referral for a prospect in a new state, I apply for this license in that state. These applications are not costly and allow me to work nationally instead of just in Georgia, where my three offices are located.

Series 65 Investment Advisor Representative

When I first started my financial services career many years ago, I only offered insurance policies. I did not want to manage clients' money or offer investments because it seemed too risky. However, as I gained experience and knowledge, I earned my broker's license and could manage portfolios for my clients. Working on the investing side allowed me to offer more opportunities to clients and to expand my income. You may or may not be offering investment services currently. I would urge you to give this serious consideration as you open your independent agency.

There are several licensing pathways for investment brokers. My recommendation is that you obtain a Series 65 License, provided by the Securities and Exchange Commission (SEC) and administered by each state. This license allows you to discuss tax implications with your clients. You must be careful not to act as a Certified Public Accountant (CPA) or tax professional, but you can examine the tax implications of various investment vehicles with clients and prospects if you have a Series 65 License. The Series 65 License requires that you act as a fiduciary, always focusing on the best interests of your client, not on your profits or commissions. This fiduciary licensing is very attractive to prospects and provides an important measure of trust.

As people age, tax implications become increasingly crucial to their investment strategies. Investors in their early adult years focus primarily on accumulation and growth. When investors begin to withdraw funds from their investments in their sixties and seventies, care is required to ensure that those withdrawals do not push them into a high tax bracket. If you cannot discuss tax implications because you lack a Series 65 License, it will be difficult for you to give your clients the best financial advice.

It is possible to have investment clients in other states as well. Under the De Minimis Rule, a financial advisor may serve up to five clients in each state without being Series 65-licensed in that state. However, there are a couple of states that will require registration before you solicit even one client. Currently these states are: Louisiana, Nebraska, New Hampshire and Texas. As you grow your independent agency to include additional advisors, they can each serve up to five clients in other states as long as they operate within the De Minimis Rule. Once you exceed five investment clients in an outside state, you will need to pursue the non-resident version of a Series 65 license for that particular state.

Note: This information is correct and current as of June 2019. Please keep abreast of changing laws and regulations on this and all licensing matters.

Broker Licensing

The Financial Industry Regulatory Authority, Inc. (FINRA) administers the broker license. FINRA is a non-governmental, private corporation which regulates brokerage firms and exchange markets, including the New York Stock Exchange. I was licensed as a broker under FINRA while still working in a captive environment. Under that license, I could offer IRAs and other non-qualified vehicles. However, I could never discuss tax implications.

When I initially opened my independent agency in 2009, I maintained my broker's license, even though I quickly obtained a Series 65 license as well. I assumed that the more licenses I had, the better it would be for my credibility. However, I soon learned that complying with the requirements of both the Series 65 and a FINRA license was a nightmare. FINRA regulations are exceptionally stringent, especially on marketing activities.

FMOs, RIAs, and BDs

In the captive environment, your parent company provides you a list of products you can market and trains you to use them effectively. Most parent companies also provide your marketing materials and manage compliance. When you become an independent advisor, you can select from many different products and are responsible for learning about them. You may be able to create your own marketing materials, and you must ensure that all your marketing complies with the regulations of your licenses. This process can be intimidating and overwhelming.

Most independent advisors join organizations which act as the middleman between advisors and companies offering financial products. These organizations provide training and reviews of marketing materials to ensure compliance. There are different types of these organizations depending upon your license.

- FMO/IMO: Field Marketing Organizations or Independent Marketing Organizations work on the insurance side. These groups work between insurance companies and independent advisors, providing training and compliance oversight. They get a small percentage of the commission from insurance products. If you are part of an FMO/IMO, you don't have to negotiate directly with insurance companies to be able to sell their products. Most of those companies prefer to deal with FMO/IMOs instead of with individual advisors.

- RIA: Registered Investment Advisor Firms work as the middleman between advisors who are Series 65-licensed and the SEC. They have agreements with recognized custodians that allow independent advisors to offer various investment vehicles. RIAs also provide training and compliance with SEC regulations.

- BD: Broker-Dealer agencies work under FINRA regulations for compliance, training, and products for licensed brokers.

As you can imagine, working with three different licenses and their regulatory agencies can be very difficult. In my early days as an independent advisor, I would prepare marketing materials and submit them to my RIA and BD, to comply with both the SEC and FINRA requirements. My RIA would quickly review the documents and make any needed corrections to ensure they were in full compliance with SEC regulations. The BD process was much more cumbersome and the FINRA rules much more difficult. Working with both agencies on the investment side of my business caused many delays and additional expenses. The fee share to the BDs was also higher than those with my RIA. In essence, maintaining both my Series 65 and broker's licenses were costing me money, time, and headaches. I dropped my broker's license after a couple of years and now operate only with the Series 65 and insurance licenses.

In my agency, we enjoy a very positive relationship with both our FMO and RIA. There are advantages to working with these organizations, including the availability of conferences and training opportunities. Additionally, when you grow your own individual or multi-advisor firm to around five million dollars of annual production, your FMO may give you marketing credits. Because we are now a high-volume firm, our FMO credits pay for the majority of our marketing expenses such as seminar and college class mailers, newspaper advertising, client events, social media expenses, and similar marketing plans.

When you first open your independent agency, you will usually work with one FMO and one RIA. As you grow your revenues, you will have more negotiating power. For example, I had one FMO for the first eight years of my business. That firm was later sold, and I needed other options, so I moved to a new FMO after extensive research. However, that FMO lacked some very important products I wanted to offer my clients. I was able to negotiate with the new FMO and add a second firm to cover the particular products that my new FMO did not offer. Over time, I moved the majority of my business to the second FMO developing a great eleven-year relationship. This second firm eventually became my primary FMO. We produce a lot of revenue for them, and they in turn assist us in many areas.

What About Residual Income?

Fiduciary advisors licensed under Series 65 cannot earn commissions on individual securities trades. Instead, they can only charge an annual account management fee. Brokers earn money on each trade and are allowed to charge trading fees and commissions. This may lead to "churning", which is the illegal practice of making numerous trades without growing a client's portfolio, just so the broker can earn the residual income. Most prospects have heard of this and are pleased to work with a Series 65 advisor who must only work in their best interests and who has no personal financial incentive to make trades.

If you are a new independent advisor, my recommendation is that you focus on your Series 65 license. If you are already independent, with a broker's license, you may be concerned about losing the residual commissions you earn on individual trades and 12b-1 fees. If that is your situation, work with a coach or mentor to determine if the benefit of those commissions outweighs the costs and possible limitations associated with your broker's license. You need to balance those commissions against building a substantial "Assets Under Management" (AUM) client book that pays residuals forever.

My experience is that for the vast majority of advisors, focusing on your Series 65 fiduciary role and insurance licenses is the best course of action. This focus will simplify your professional life. It eliminates any possible conflict of interest when you are accepting securities commissions on some trades under your broker's license and not accepting them when you are operating under your Series 65 license. And it's one less regulatory agency overseeing your work.

Compliance Is Key

Regardless of what you decide about your personal license, you must always comply with the regulations of those licenses. Our profession has been subject to much scrutiny in the past years because of the unethical behavior of a few rogue agents, brokers, and advisors. It is important to realize that all your actions, words, and marketing materials are subject to review for compliance. It is also a competitive arena where competitors may attempt to discredit you.

I've had other advisors attend my public seminars, record them, and send them to the SEC to try to get me in trouble. Other times, inspectors from the licensing board have attended those seminars to ensure I was doing the right thing. You never know when you will be evaluated, so just do the right things consistently.

There are websites like *BrokerCheck* and *Yelp* where consumers can view grievances or negative reviews of your agency. You cannot get away with bending the rules or acting outside of the law, at least not for very long.

I am proud to say that in my nearly thirty years in this industry, I've never had a written client complaint lodged or validated against me. I've built my reputation carefully to ensure that I am known as an ethical financial advisor who always focuses on client satisfaction and legal compliance. That reputation brings my agency outstanding referrals and clients of significant net worth who are very careful to vet anyone involved with their finances. It pays to know the rules, to follow them wholeheartedly, and always pay attention to your reputation in your community and industry.

It is also critical that you document EVERY prospect and client conversation and appointment. We use a dictation service known as *Mobile Assistant.* With a short five-minute phone call, advisors dictate all aspects of the conversation or appointment. In the event a prospect or client questions the relationship, you will have all your dictated notes stored into your Client Relationship Management (CRM) system. We also use *Redtail* to track and log all client information and communications.

M. Scott Moore

CHAPTER 8

SELECTING PRODUCTS

This chapter is a challenging one to write. The financial services industry is always changing and evolving. Products and platforms which are winners today could be problematic in the future. Considering this changeable industry landscape, in this chapter, you'll learn the principles behind selecting the most effective products for your clients. These principles will not change over time and will always guide you through the research process. One way to stay current on products and offerings is to have a resource of mentors to help you with selecting the best products to fulfill the needs and best interests of your clients. I do this with several advisors/mentors on a reciprocal basis.

One of the key things to remember when researching products and platforms is your fiduciary role. Anything that you suggest to your clients should be in their best interest. When you keep that principle in mind, you'll be able to sort through opportunities more efficiently.

Understanding Your Client

The age of your client is a significant consideration when selecting investment opportunities. Most brokers focus on younger earners who are building investment portfolios. These clients usually add more funds to their investment accounts. The goal for this kind of investor is to accumulate as much money as possible, which generally gives them a higher risk tolerance.

However, clients of or nearing retirement age generally do not continue to add to their investments, so their goals are usually different. Most clients preparing for, or already retired, want to preserve their portfolios with the ability to withdraw funds regularly. Their focus is not solely on growth, but on preservation and the ability to access their funds.

Standard industry practice is to invest all retirement funds in vehicles that carry some risk and then manage that risk. Consumers are urged to use portfolios with a mixture of high-, medium-, and low-risk vehicles depending on both their tolerance for risk and their investment goals. However, as the market downturns in both 2001 and 2008 demonstrated, even low-risk investments can lose money, sometimes quite significantly. These losses are particularly dangerous for older clients who are no longer earning or contributing to their investments. Even a 30% loss can be quite devastating for clients who must withdraw from their investments for either monthly living needs or unforeseen emergencies, such as assisting a child or grandchild with unplanned medical or legal expenses. In these situations, it may be challenging to recoup those market losses.

I employ a different strategy for my retired or near-term retiree clients, who constitute the majority of my roster. In my almost twenty years as a mutual fund broker and ten years as a fiduciary advisor, I've found that the most prudent and successful investment strategy for retirees and near-term retirees combines a mixture of safe, foundational vehicles with principal protection, coupled with the balance of their investments in a carefully managed risk strategy.

For example, let's imagine I have a client who is older than fifty-five, with one million dollars to invest. In this scenario, I may suggest that a portion of the money be placed in a no-risk foundational investment to drive their future income needs while preserving their principal. Then the balance may be invested to match their risk tolerance, ensuring that, in the event of an actual market downturn, the client experiences only a tolerable loss before their funds are repositioned or moved out of harm's way. Each client needs individual guidance based on their financial assets, risk tolerance, and income needs to determine the best mix for their retirement portfolio.

This type of mixed investment strategy creates efficient portfolios with reasonable growth over time, along with some asset protection for retired investors. Many brokers push back against this non-traditional strategy as it reduces their ongoing fees and extra revenue. Brokers usually earn more than fiduciary advisors over time if all investments are placed in the risk category, as they receive ongoing fees for those types of portfolios.

The Moore's Wealth Management (MWM) Strategy

For most clients aged fifty-five and above, use a mixture of low fee vehicles in these two categories:

1. Safe Side: Foundational vehicles with asset protection. Many of these products have no fees. In some cases where a client has unique needs, such as the need for immediate access to the funds, it may be worth paying a modest fee, but most clients can use "no fee" platforms. These are often insurance vehicles with asset protection, such as fixed or fixed index annuities.

2. Risk Side: Exchange Traded Funds (ETFs) coupled with individual stocks if desired. ETFs generally have low fees, in large part because many do not have active fund managers. These can be much more cost-effective investment vehicles compared to most mutual funds, especially if they are properly structured.

Fees

The word "fee" is the most hated word in our industry. Ten years ago, consumers paid investment fees without thinking about them. Today, due in large part to advertising and public consumer education, consumers are looking for the lowest fees possible. That's a reasonable expectation. My clients are willing to pay a fair fee if they understand that I have done the research and found them the best option.

When I sold mutual funds years ago, I did not realize that most variable annuities and mutual funds have higher fees than advertised. These are often not listed in the client's statements. They are found only in the prospectus. According to an article in Forbes magazine, "The Undisclosed Fees in Mutual Funds," many mutual funds have additional fees not detailed in the prospectus. These are the trading costs, which are not standardized and therefore, not listed in places where your clients will see them.

I sold mutual funds for almost twenty years before I learned this information so it may be new to you as well. If you are considering an investment vehicle, look for the many hidden fees such as trading costs, cash drag, and phantom income tax it often generates. Be cautious, since they do not appear in the prospectus.

Whether you are selecting vehicles for the safe side or investments for the risk side of any portfolio, do your research and select vehicles with the lowest possible fees. I avoid variable annuities and most mutual funds because of their high fee structure. Many mutual funds have hidden fees, most of which are passed on to the consumer, as well as a fee to the manager.

Beware of Tax Implications

Brokers cannot legally discuss tax planning with clients unless they are tax certified, which most are not. Some mutual funds can have adverse tax consequences for consumers, referred to as phantom income tax on non-qualified investments, even when the investment does not grow. As a fiduciary advisor, you may discuss tax implications if you state that you are not a CPA or tax attorney, if indeed you are not. It is wise to talk with your client about the tax implications of their investment choices, especially during the "distribution years" of their retirement. Part of my mentoring program is to educate advisors about how the lack of essential information can cause grave negative financial impacts for their clients.

Finding Investment Opportunities

Advisors can access funds, insurance policies, and investment vehicles in two places. FMOs can provide referrals to RIA firms which offer multiple investment vehicles to advisors and their clients. However, that usually means that the FMO becomes a middleman and typically receives a portion of the investment fees, which increases your cost as an advisor as well as the cost to the client.

Some independent advisors act as their own RIA, negotiating directly with custodians to avoid paying override fees to FMOs, but they take on much greater legal risks and liabilities as well as compliance and billing costs in that role.

I do not suggest this course of action, primarily because it places significant risk on the independent advisor. Obviously, investments can be volatile, no matter what safeguards are in place. Some investors may become upset and possibly initiate a lawsuit when their investments lose money. Even if you have done everything correctly, with full documentation, you may still incur legal defense fees if you are working as an RIA.

Also, if you decide to become an RIA, you must either hire a compliance officer or pay a compliance firm to track all your marketing and ensure that it follows the law. That compliance officer or firm also handles all monthly or quarterly client billing. These services can be very costly and complicated.

Instead, I suggest working under an RIA (as an Investment Advisor Representative (IAR)) who charges low fees for quality services. When you do this, the RIA monitors compliance, handles all billing, and provides a layer of protection in the case of lawsuits. It took me nearly ten years as an independent advisor (and almost thirty years in the financial industry) to find a low-cost, full-service RIA. My mentoring program includes assistance with RIA selection.

New independent advisors, especially if they came from a captive environment that directed which products they could offer, may be confused and overwhelmed by this information. I understand. Over the years, I did extensive research, visiting the offices of the leading RIA firms in the US to find the best one for my clients. I got on a plane and flew to each firm because I wanted to speak to their leadership instead of just reading their marketing materials. As I mentioned, I discovered an outstanding RIA with very reasonable fees which is an exceptional opportunity for my investors. My advisors and I continue to monitor the marketplace to ensure we are working with the best RIA and FMO firms.

Strategic Client Selection

It is essential to research the investment vehicles you offer clients, and it is just as important to carefully consider the types of clients you wish to serve. Some independent advisors do not serve clients with less than one hundred thousand dollars to invest. In my experience, clients with less money to invest usually have a lower tolerance for risk. They may become fearful during market downturns, requiring more support from you. They are also ineligible for some investment vehicles, especially those with the lowest fees that require a high initial investment.

I've also learned that potential clients who are argumentative and combative during the initial stages, rarely become more cooperative after making investments. It will drain your resources of time and emotional strength to work with this type of client. When I first began working as an independent advisor, I took on any client who came to me. While I learn from every client I sit down with, I have also learned that some clients are not only unpleasant but also unprofitable for my firm and me.

My recommendation is that you create a standard or a policy about the types of clients you will accept. If you wish to serve a few clients with lower net worth, you may, as long as you have enough clients who invest at a higher level to balance them out. Most of your client base should have at a minimum between one hundred thousand to two-hundred fifty thousand dollars to invest to ensure the best use of your time and to gain maximum profits. When you are careful about your client selection process, you will enjoy working with your clients more and trust that as their funds grow, so will your profits.

TIP: *As a mentor, I offer periodic webinars and workshops which provide updates on specific financial products and the most current successful vehicles I use with my clients. Go to ScottMooreConsulting. com and register for the notification list for my next training opportunity.*

M. Scott Moore

CHAPTER 9

YOUR TRANSITION PLAN FROM CAPTIVE TO INDEPENDENT ADVISOR

Now that you understand the big picture of how leaving your captive environment can give you financial freedom, you know the personal characteristics you need, and which licenses you need to grow your business, it's time to get practical. I used this roadmap for my transition from captive to independent advisor. My recommendation is that you follow this roadmap to ensure you do not miss any crucial steps and to avoid wasting time.

1. **Develop a Clear Concise Mental Picture (CCMP)**. Begin with the end in mind. Everything starts with a clear picture of where you want to be in the future. Think about what your agency will look like in five years:

   - How much business do you want to manage?
   - How large is your staff?
   - What is your personal annual income?
   - What type of clientele do you wish to serve?
   - What message does the appearance of your office send to visitors?
   - Are you involved in your community?

- What percentage of your business comes from referrals?
- How do you attract new clients?

2. **Select a promising location.** I did a lot of research before selecting my location in Gainesville, Georgia. I did not live in that area but knew that Atlanta was a growing city with many young professionals. I wanted to be located near Atlanta to market to those professionals as well as to any of their parents who moved to the area to be closer to grandchildren. Today, 80% of my clients are not from Georgia but have moved here to retire.

I also researched medical care. Retirees want access to excellent medical centers. Gainesville has a top-rated hospital, recognized at the state and national level. Located on a sizable lake, Gainesville has a large population of retirees and those with high net worth. At that time, it was a small city with a hometown feel, which appealed to my personality. I wanted a place small enough to minimize competition, where I could capitalize on my friendly nature. I was already licensed in Georgia and understood the state regulations.

Once I toured Gainesville, I discovered the downtown area featured office space in historic buildings. Because many local professionals had been in one particular historic office building for over twenty years, being in that type of office would suggest mine was a trustworthy and traditional agency. This perception is essential when dealing with retirees and near-term retirees, my target market.

While I did not move to Gainesville, I was able to commute there from our home outside Atlanta. It is possible to open a successful firm in a community where you do not reside. Today, I have a corporate apartment in Gainesville where I stay part of the week. I work from my mountain lake home in North Carolina the rest of the time.

3. **Select your company name and register it with the state**. Solicit help from a local attorney and CPA. Get your logo designed. Register the domain name for your future website.

4. **Get your securities Series 65 license in addition to your Life/Health Insurance license.**

5. **Locate a small four-room office.** You don't have to move in immediately but determine the location right away so you can tell prospects exactly where your new office will be when it opens. This clear visual picture will help prospects feel comfortable, knowing precisely where they will come to meet with you. It will also give you confidence. I suggest four rooms so that in the future, you can expand to add an advisor without moving.

I do not recommend using shared office space. It sends a message that you lack capital and are not serious about your success, especially in those facilities with shared receptionists and no permanent office assignments. You will send a much better message when you have your own office space.

6. **Determine if your current firm has you in a non-compete agreement and review it with an attorney**. Most restrict the advisor from work within a 50-mile geographical radius from your current firm's office location for a two-year period. This rule does not usually apply to any investment securities business if your current clients ask you for advice. Have those clients sign a letter regarding this, for your protection. Most companies aggressively work to enforce non-compete agreements related to their current insurance policies since those generate ongoing and very profitable premiums/revenue.

7. **Once you are ready to make the transition, stop writing business at your current firm**. If you don't have much money saved, go on a ninety-day activity blitz to double your

standard results and cash flow. Save all the extra income for your independent agency.

8. Save all referral contacts for your new venture.

9. Determine the best date to leave your current employer. Make sure it will provide you with the highest legal and financial benefits. For example, if you receive monthly or quarterly deferred compensation or earnings that will discontinue, consider resigning after the next large payout.

10. Have the new FMO begin your background checks and provide product training materials before you resign so you can begin to study for the exams. Note, check first to ensure this will comply with the laws of your state.

11. If necessary due to financial limitations, plan to work three to six months without an office as I did. Work out of your home or car while you see referral prospects.

12. Research and interview multiple independent FMOs to determine the best one for you. My mentoring program has already researched almost all of the FMOs in existence to determine the best one(s) available.

13. Contact all your clients to let them know you are going independent, and that you will no longer be limited on the products and services you can offer. Remind them that you have always told them you have given them the best products and services to your knowledge and that *if something better came along, you would let them know.* This message allows for continued appreciation from your clients and does not give the appearance of instability. My wife, Carla, reminded me of this promise and suggested that I "re-communicate" it to my clients when announcing my new status. It was quite effective as I never received any negative responses.

14. **Only move current clients to your new services if it is in their best interest, and if they write and sign a letter that they contacted you.** When they do call, have a form letter ready that they can sign, stating that they contacted you for assistance. These letters will be vital if you have any issues with your non-compete clause.

15. **Once you have a date to sign your new office lease, be sure to budget three hundred to four hundred dollars a week for a twenty to twenty-five hour per week part-time assistant so you will not have to answer the phone or greet people at the door.** Most people will not consider investing or doing any significant financial transactions with an agent who does not have the structure and perceived financial stability that comes with having a staff. In the beginning, you can work with a part-time assistant who will cover the office when you have client appointments. You can hire a stay-at-home mother, a college intern, or retiree at reasonable prices. Just be sure they have a professional manner and the ability to appropriately welcome people into the office.

16. **Plan for an initial budget of $25,000 to open your office.**

    • $1,000 to join the National Ethics Association (NEA) and the local Chamber of Commerce
    • $2,000 for three used desks and office chairs, a 42-inch round table, and three chairs to place in your office or the fourth office
    • $1,000 for two laptops
    • $500 for a printer/fax/scanner with a multi-sheet feeder
    • $200 for a small refrigerator for drinks and water
    • $100 for a coffee maker

- $400 for general office supplies, business cards, letterhead and envelopes
- $1,000 deposit for a 12-month office lease. Never sign an extended lease until you are sure the location will work for you
- $10,000 for two mailers, four seminars, and two marketing campaigns
- $5,000 for your first two months of basic office expenses and rent
- $500 for a securities Series 65 errors and omissions (E&O) insurance
- $3,000 for installation of a phone line, a phone system, internet service, a basic website, and miscellaneous expenses

17. **Plan on a monthly operating budget of $2,500 for recurring office expenses**:

- $1,000 for office rent and utilities
- $1,150 for a part-time assistant
- $200 for the office phone with three lines (two phone lines plus a fax line) and high-speed internet
- $100 to lease a small multi-line expandable business phone system with 3 to 4 handsets
- Approximately $50 to have a professional website maintained by a 3rd party company

18. **Consider your personal income needs to determine your net financial investment.** You will need $25,000 to open the office, another $5,000 to cover your first two months of recurring office expenses, plus enough money to cover two months of living expenses if you are the sole provider for your family.

19. **Interview and select an excellent low-cost, high-benefit RIA firm and secure the Series 65 securities license as**

soon as possible if you don't already have it. I can be of assistance. My mentoring program introduces advisors to the best value FMO and RIA in the industry.

20. **Build professional relationships within your new community, especially with CPAs and attorneys, to present joint public seminars and cultivate reciprocal referrals.** This process may require several years to prove yourself. Local established professionals will first need to see stability and growth in your business before they trust you with referrals.

21. **Once your new office is open, shift your appointments away from meeting in clients' homes and invite them to your office.** This change will minimize your windshield time and maximize your productivity.

This office mindset is a major paradigm shift for most advisors. Most of us were trained to see prospects and clients at their kitchen table. However, when you meet in a person's home, their comfort zone, they are in control and call the shots. When you shift your client meetings to your office, the dynamic will change. You'll be recognized as the meeting leader. Other professionals such as attorneys, dentists, lawyers, and physicians do not go to clients' homes. People respect them enough to go to their place of business. You want the same level of respect for yourself and your new agency.

M. Scott Moore

CHAPTER 10

A ROADMAP FOR REVITALIZING AND GROWING AN EXISTING INDEPENDENT AGENCY

If you are reading this book and already own an independent financial firm, you'll be able to use all the material in this book. However, your roadmap to success will be a little shorter because you are already working independently and have your office and clientele. If you are reading this book while still in the captive environment, this list will give you an idea of how you can grow your agency after your first year.

I'll cover all the tasks on this list in detail in subsequent chapters. This chapter is a broad overview of what to do. Read on, and you'll discover how to do it effectively. Note that I use the pronoun "him" for easy reading. You can recruit male or female associate advisors. Gender is not as important as the skills and work ethic of your trainees.

- Develop the mindset that not all potential advisors are a headache to train and work with, nor will they always leave you. If you have some past negative experiences with recruiting, I'm going to show you how to do it successfully because building a team is paramount to reaching your financial goals.

- Decide on the business structure you want such as LLC, Inc., etc. Discuss the options with your CPA and attorney.

- You must be the "master-copy" for training so begin to document a system for all of your sales activities that others can follow.

- Recruit one advisor at a time so that you can stay in your current office for another year.

- Research and understand the importance of succession planning and consider younger advisors working first as associates/associate advisors.

- Recruit a potential associate advisor. Start by having him design and prepare prospect cases so he can learn from a technical role.

- After twelve months in a technical support role, train your potential associate in your sales processes and have him teach the next recruit his former job as a case preparation specialist.

- Create a twelve to thirty-six-month multi-step training process to ease your new advisor into his role to build his confidence. Introduce him to clients when he is ready.

- Provide ongoing feedback to the new advisor after each of his presentations, sales calls, or seminars.

- Offer group health, dental, vision insurance, and 401(k) plans with your firm paying 50-65% of the premiums to encourage loyalty.

- Create a Client Advisory Council by selecting ten of your top clients who have been with you at least two years. Do not only pick the clients with the most significant accounts. You want to choose clients who are very happy with you and your services, can influence others, and would enjoy becoming your biggest cheerleaders.

- Create a client reference list with at least six clients on it and indicate the year they began with you. Prospects want to speak to a diverse group of your clients, including a few who have been with you the longest. As your firm grows, you need three separate client reference lists: Standard, High Net Worth (over one million dollars in assets), and Widows.

- Once you have one associate advisor and full-time assistant, begin to host one major client appreciation event per year. My mentoring program teaches all of the specifics for a successful client appreciation event.

- Begin to give back to your local community by supporting local charities or hosting community events.

- Consider opening a second satellite office in another community. If you use shared office space, ensure that you never leave client files there overnight, so you won't need to register that office with your RIA firm and state regulators.

- Brand your name by placing articles in local magazines or in the local newspaper (retirees still desire and enjoy reading the paper) related to your firm.

- After two years of branding work, use the media to market your work. Expand your mailer and social media campaigns now that your community is aware of your services.

- Once you have two solidly qualified advisors, that you personally trained who are working independently, get your firm valued by a certified valuation professional and create a succession plan with ownership opportunities. Getting to this point may take five to six years. But it is key to obtaining loyalty from your advisors whom you have already spent a LOT of time training.

- Create a succession and vesting plan to allow for your eventual exit from the agency.

M. Scott Moore

CHAPTER 11

BUILDING YOUR AGENCY'S POSITIVE REPUTATION

When you move into your new location, you must remember that nobody knows you. You are no longer wrapped in the blanket of your former parent company. It's just you and the name of your new business. Starting out fresh is a golden opportunity, so be very intentional about how you want the community to view both your business and you as a person.

Realize that people are skeptical of newcomers and new businesses. Many business ventures fail within the first five years. People don't want to risk their life savings with a financial advisor whose firm appears unstable. When I opened Moore's Wealth Management in a small city in Georgia, I had considerable obstacles to overcome. I was an outsider in an area where the good-old-boy network was a way of life. I knew I'd have to work much harder than a local to win trust and attract clients.

One of the first things I did was to find an office in one of the most traditional/historic buildings in town. Built in 1901, stable tenants had occupied this landmark for many years. It was a classic building right in the center of the downtown area. I chose it because I knew my clients were very traditional and would feel most comfortable in a conventional setting. I also wanted a space in which we could expand as our business grew. We are still in that location eleven years later. We've expanded our offices several times but stay in our original location to highlight our stability. While many advisors grow to buy their own office building, I decided to continue to lease space in the most well-known building on the square in Gainesville.

Carla and I furnished the office with care. We did not have enough money to buy nice furniture for the reception area, so we took the furniture out of our living room at home. It was important that people could sit in a comfortable home-like office instead of a cold, sterile room with uncomfortable chairs like those in a dentist's office.

We put up lots of family photos including those of our parents and grandparents, and their military service pictures. Our goal was to send the message that we were traditional people who would treat clients as if they were part of our family. We always had coffee, tea, hot chocolate, soft drinks, waters, and cookies available. Carla got an old-fashioned glass candy dish and kept it filled with Ghirardelli chocolates. We could have saved a few dollars with less expensive chocolates but wanted to send a message of pampering and welcome.

I grew up respecting the "golden rule" of treating others as I expected to be treated, so our logo was designed featuring a knight in shining armour on a horse with the tagline: "Protecting Your Future". A few years into our business, we expanded and added a large conference room. Carla found a seven-foot metal sculpture of a medieval knight which we placed in the new conference room. I thought it was a little silly, but I was wrong as most people comment on that statue when they enter the conference room.

Everything from our letterhead to the furnishings in the office is designed to appeal to retirees and near-term retirees looking for a safe, stable business to protect their hard-earned retirement funds. I am fortunate that Carla is very creative and helped me design a visual look for the agency which clearly demonstrates our values.

Today you'll hear things about the client experience. That wasn't a catchphrase ten years ago. However, I realized that I had to have a solid plan that would build trust with every client interaction. From the first call or meeting to ongoing client management, I designed everything to engender trust and demonstrate stability. This process took time, but over a few years, incredible growth was the reward for my efforts. I lay this out in detail in my mentoring program.

It Starts with You

Trust is the ultimate objective of anyone in sales. If you can gain the trust of prospects and get them to like you, you have won 90% of the battle.

Likability and trust build solid relationships that last and can even withstand a few inadvertent mistakes along the way. It isn't enough to have a welcoming office, inspiring logo, or outstanding knowledge of your products and services. If people don't like you personally, they will not invest their money with you. You must live the ethics and values of your firm, every single day.

When I opened the office, I was acutely aware that people would be curious about me since I was a newcomer. I made sure that every time I went to a store, restaurant, or Chamber of Commerce meeting, I dressed professionally, and acted friendly and humble. I did not want to send the message that I thought I was better than anyone else, but that I was sincere in my desire to serve the people of the community.

I also trained myself never to get angry when someone came in with a complaint or a chip on their shoulders. My Type A, engineering personality would have me respond to fire with fire, but that is no way to win trust. Instead, I always apologized immediately and then worked tirelessly to find a solution that would please the prospect or client. I'd say, "Mr. Smith, I am so sorry. These types of things rarely happen in our business, but when they do, I want to do everything in my power to make you happy."

I trained my staff to react in the same way, apologizing quickly for any errors or inconveniences regardless of who was at fault. If someone arrived for an appointment and I could not see them at precisely the scheduled time, my receptionist would apologize that I was running late, offer more refreshments, and let people know I'd be with them in the next few minutes. I learned to manage my appointments carefully so I can be on time and rarely make people wait.

Engage Your Current Clients

It's a dirty little secret in our industry that many advisors skip doing annual reviews for existing clients. Many advisors are so busy selling to new clients that more senior clients can become ignored and feel unappreciated.

Faithfully conducting annual reviews is one of the best ways to develop an ongoing, positive relationship with clients. Clients appreciate the personal touch and assurances that you are watching their portfolio. Whether you recommend changes or that they maintain their current investments, always invest the time to do those reviews. Today, we serve over six hundred clients, and every one of them has a yearly reassessment. Most of these are conducted in our office, but we use the telephone or computer for clients who are out of state.

During that review, ask for referrals of friends and professional contacts. New networking opportunities can develop from your clients' accountants, attorneys and property/casualty agents. Tell your clients that you love working with them and would love referrals to other wonderful people like themselves. My mentoring program lays out specific processes and strategies to ensure that referrals are a constant stream of opportunities and ongoing revenue.

It's also important to invite your current clients to all of your public events, especially your dinner seminars. Many advisors wonder why they would pay meal expenses for existing clients at these events when the objective is to secure new clients. That is short-sighted thinking. When you invite long-term clients to public affairs, you have a built-in cheering squad. New prospects can ask questions about what it's like to work with you and get a favorable report from happy clients. I try to have at least one current client at every table during my dinner seminars and public workshops. We print up name tags for all these clients who attend the event and scatter them around the tables to ensure they are placed strategically to influence the prospects sitting nearby.

Existing clients enjoy knowing you are still interested in them and want to give them an enjoyable evening out. They will hear your message again and remember why they chose your firm in the first place. If they were starting to doubt you or considering moving to another company, attending your event will keep them in your business. If you are in a small city as I am, many of your existing clients will know your prospects and enjoy visiting with them. Prospects are delighted to see that people they know invest with you, which is another subtle way of establishing trust.

I always invite my existing clients to bring a friend or another couple along if they like. It's an easy way to get more referrals. Even if your clients don't wish to bring anyone, I ensure that the invitation makes it clear that I am looking forward to seeing them and want them to attend the event.

Once you finish your presentation, you can leave the room and let all your guests talk, knowing that you have happy clients in the room who will sing your praises. I've had a prospect say to me at his appointment after a dinner seminar, "Let me tell you why I came in after your seminar the other night. You are so confident in the trust your clients have in you that you left the room. You left us with your clients. Nobody does that. And your clients were so grateful for what you've done for them, that I had to come in and see you myself." That kind of word of mouth praise from existing clients is more valuable than gold.

I communicate with my clients every month, either with a printed or electronic newsletter. The newsletter provides useful information, a calendar of upcoming events, and sometimes education on a topic of interest to them. These monthly communications remind people that I care about them, that our agency is growing and thriving, and that they can feel comfortable investing with us.

Use the Media Wisely

For the first two years, I placed ads in the local newspaper on a regular basis. My goal was to ensure that everyone in the area heard about our business. After two years, a colleague told me I needed to start the second phase of a media campaign. We already had name recognition. Next, we needed to educate people about what we did.

Our local paper did not have a financial column. So, I went to the editor and offered to write one every week at no charge. They ran in the Sunday paper. This kind of article is called an advertorial, and it was tremendously successful. The goal was to provide useful information. I'd write about how to save money for college, how to teach your children or grandchildren about saving, different types of investments, IRAs, and other financial topics. It did not matter if the subject of the article was not immediately useful to my target market of retirees. This exposure positioned me as the local financial expert who was generous with his knowledge. I wrote these articles for two years, and years later, they continue to lead to new prospects.

Be Unique

After living a couple of years in Gainesville, one of my clients gave me a terrific idea. She previously resided in Florida and participated in a monthly dance sponsored by a financial advisor and a restaurant. I immediately went to a restaurant that served great food, where I was already doing a lot of business. We developed the "50-Plus Dancing Diners," a monthly dance we co-sponsored. The restaurant created a special discounted menu for the evening, and I paid for a live band. I invited all of my clients and prospects in the monthly newsletter. Carla and I, and the full staff attended and did our best to make sure everyone had a wonderful time.

During the event, the restaurant owner would come out and talk about the success of Moore's Wealth Management. I would speak about the fabulous food and atmosphere of the restaurant. It was a win-win. We collected people's email addresses with the promise that we would never market to them but would invite them to future dances. We'd have great music, excellent ten to fifteen-dollar dinner discounts, and a raffle where I'd give the winners fifty-dollar gift cards. People loved these events. They had a lot of fun, there was no sales presentation, and they were eager to return for future dances.

These events were such a sensation that the local newspaper came to take photos and interview me. The reporter asked me why I was spending money every month to sponsor these dances. I answered that the community welcomed us so beautifully when we opened our office, that I wanted to give back. I said, "Listen, I'm not from here. I opened this firm in 2009, and this community welcomed me with open arms. I want people to know that we are here, we care, and we always will strive to give back." The article gave an excellent history of the business, my background, and even about my family.

The article was wonderfully positive and built additional goodwill in the community. Somehow, Forbes Magazine got a copy of the article and called, asking to interview me about how Moore's Wealth Management sponsored dances to give back to the community. One of the premier financial magazines in the country featured our Georgia firm, because of those dances.

Taking a risk to invest time and money into a community event may seem scary when you are a new business struggling to grow. However, if you select your events wisely, you will reap the benefits money cannot buy, such as significant name recognition, word of mouth advertising from delighted clients and participants, and media coverage. Being featured in a news story gets you much more mileage than placing a traditional advertisement in the paper. Giving back to your community is one of the best ways to build your business and your likability at the same time.

Historic Hosch Building...1901

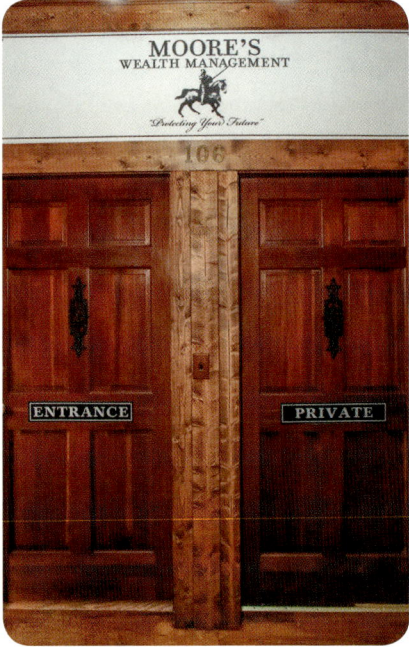

Moore's Wealth Management Suite 106

Gainesville, GA Square

Moore's Wealth Management Reception

"Protecting Your Future"

Business Builder of the Year 2012

Moore's Wealth Management Main Conference Room

Scott and Carla Moore Family History

Moore's Wealth Management

Carla and Scott Moore cut ribbon at Moore's Wealth Management, a seasoned financial advisory firm with a focus on a fiduciary level of service. Located in Gainesville and Alpharetta, the firm recently doubled the size of their main office in Gainesville due to business growth. Scott Moore, founder and senior advisor, was recognized as Advisor of the Year for 2011 and 2012 by one of the top independent advisor organizations in the country. Scott was formerly a mutual fund broker for one of the largest investment companies on Wall Street. Moore's Wealth Management takes a conservative approach to protecting and preserving clients' retirement assets and has a low-risk, safe and secure investment philosophy toward managing client's portfolios, representing some of the top private wealth mangers in the U.S. To show appreciation for clients and the community, the firm hosted an open house in April. The Greater Hall Chamber, along with hundreds of the firm's clients and guests celebrated with a ribbon cutting ceremony. Moore's Wealth Management, 210 Washington Street NW, Suite 106, Gainesville, GA 30501. 770-535-5000. *mooreswealthmanagement.com*

Investment advice is offered by Horter Investment Management, LLC, a Registered Investment Adviser. Insurance and annuity products are sold separately through Moore's Wealth Management, LLC. Securities transactions for Horter Investment Management clients are placed through Pershing Advisor Solutions, Trust Company of America, Jefferson National Monument Advisor, Fidelity, and Security Benefit Life.

Congratulations!
Thank You for Your Support!

GREATER HALL
CHAMBER OF COMMERCE

Moore's Wealth Management Client Advisory Council Meeting

M. Scott Moore Advisor of the Year 2012

My Sister's Place Sunset Soiree
April 25, 2013

The dinner-dance at the Chattahoochee Country Club is the annual fund-raiser for the Gainesville-based nonprofit that provides shelter for homeless women and mothers with children.
Far left: Georgia senator Butch Miller, left, and Gov. Nathan Deal pose for a photo at the soiree.
Left: Deborah Mack smiles for the camera.

Photos by Simpson Custom Photography

Left: The staff of Moore's Wealth Management pose for a photo at the soiree before dinner service.

Below: Music for the evening was provided by Peggie Hoskins and the SoulShine Band.

Right: Select items were auctioned off to benefit My Sister's Place during the annual fundraiser. Darla Eden graciously played Vanna White for the evening.

Spouses and Advisors of Moore's Wealth Management attend annual fundraiser for "My Sister's Place" to support the community.

103

Moore's Wealth Management

Gainesvil

MOORE'S WEALTH MANAGEMENT ANNUAL CLIENT APPRECIATION EVENT

Held at the Chattahoochee Country Club

SCOTT MOORE, FOUNDER AND SENIOR ADVISOR of Moore's Wealth Management, has been in the financial services industry for over 20 years and has developed 100's of clients throughout the Southeast. He has a low-risk, safe & secure philosophy toward managing his client's retirement assets while providing a reasonable annualized rate of return over 5-10-15 years with some of the finest Private Wealth Managers in the country. Because of this philosophy, Moore's Wealth Management has seen continued growth and success throughout 2012. Due to tremendous growth in the North Georgia area, Moore's Wealth Management has recently doubled the size of their Gainesville office and increased staffing in that location. The family owned company is growing at a rate of 75-100 clients/yr and is expected to exceed this growth in 2013 with the addition of another full time Independent Fiduciary Advisor, Mark Peterson.

Scott was a mutual fund broker with one of the largest investment firms on Wall Street for almost 17 years before becoming an Independent Fiduciary Advisor about four years ago. Having been on both sides of the profession, he can quickly analyze a client's retirement portfolio to determine if it was designed for their best interest or the best interest of their financial professional. As a fiduciary, Scott is held to a much higher professional standard than a typical broker. He has been nationally recognized as an "Ed Slott Master Elite IRA Advisor" where there are fewer than 260 members across the nation. Scott was also recognized with the distinguished "Advisor of the Year" award or 2011 from one of the top Independent advisor organizations in the country. He is a skilled financial professional who utilizes the latest estate planning and investment techniques to design and implement personalized strategies that can help reduce financial risk, lower taxes, avoid probate, and protect assets from nursing home costs. Scott's offices are located in Alpharetta and Gainesville, Georgia, where he and his two older sons, Chris and Brian, enjoy serving others in their growing financial family business.

Scott and his wife of 31 years, Carla, have five children ranging in age from 18 to 30 and four wonderful grandchildren. In his spare time, Scott enjoys spending time with his family and attending automotive enthusiast events as well as restoring classic cars. Scott and his wife, Carla, also love to cruise the Georgia Mountains on their motorcycle.

For more information on how Scott may be able to serve you and your family, please call one of our offices at (770) 535-5000 or (678) 566-3590.

Times Newspaper Article
12 Senior Prom

M Wealth Management held their Annual Client Appreciation Event themed -

"As Time Goes By"
A Senior Prom
The Event was held September 29th at the beautiful Chattahoochee Country Club. There were almost 200 clients and guests in attendance. It was an evening of live music, dancing, great food and fabulous door prizes!

Mark & Liz Peterson, new additions to Moore's Wealth Management

OORE'S
MANAGEMENT

y Your Future"

LOCATIONS:

210 Washington St., NW • Suite 106
Gainesville, GA 30501

12600 Deerfield Pkwy • Suite 100
Alpharetta, GA 30004

www.mooreswealthmanagement.com

FREQUENTLY ASKED QUESTIONS

WHO WOULD BENEFIT FROM A MEETING?
• Anyone who is looking for an unbiased evaluation of their current financial situation to ensure their best possible position.
• Anyone with an IRA, 401K, TSA, or any other investment, who would like to fully understand what they own and how to maximize these dollars.
• Anyone who would like a plan to bring certainty to their financial goals.

IS MOORE'S WEALTH MANAGEMENT LIMITED TO SPECIFIC INVESTMENT COMPANIES?
• No. Scott Moore started his investment firm because he believes that each investor is unique and no single investment company is right for everyone.
• Moore's Wealth Management has access to the entire universe of investment products without limitation so we can help clients get the most value for their dollar.

I ALREADY WORK WITH A FINANCIAL REPRESENTATIVE WHY DO I NEED TO SEE SCOTT?
• Ninety percent of the people who come in to visit with us already have a financial representative. Many times that representative is not a retirement planning specialist, and more often than not, that person works for a particular company rather than for the client.

HOW DO I SCHEDULE A TIME TO VISIT WITH SCOTT?
• You may schedule a time to visit by calling our Gainesville office at 770-535-5000 or our Alpharetta office at 678-566-3590.

WHAT ARE THE OFFICE HOURS?
• By appointment.
• We are normally available Monday – Friday, 9:00 – 5:00

WHAT ARE MY OBLIGATIONS FOR MY FREE FACE-TO-FACE VISIT?
• There is absolutely no charge or obligation.
• Your first visit is designed to answer your questions, give you ample information to decide if we can help you, and that's it.
• You decide if you want to meet us again, and there is NEVER A FEE FOR OUR TIME!

WHAT IS THE CHARGE FOR SUBSEQUENT MEETINGS?
• There is NEVER any charge for our time.
• Different programs have different fee structures, all of which we will help you fully understand before proceeding.

WHAT SHOULD I BRING TO THE FACE-TO-FACE MEETING?
    The following items would be helpful, if you wish to bring them:
• Your latest financial statements such as: Mutual funds, CD's, Life Insurance policies, annuity policies, retirement accounts (IRA, 401K, TSA, 403B, etc.) [Please bring your statements not just a spreadsheet]
• Wills and Trusts
• A copy of your most recent Federal Income Tax Return
• An estimate of your annual expenses
• Any questions you may want to write down for discussion

WHAT HAPPENS DURING THE FACE-TO-FACE MEETING?
• This is YOUR hour. WE will answer and address any questions you may have.
• By reviewing your information, Scott will better understand your financial concerns and can then provide recommendations.
• At the close of the hour, you will decide if you want to meet again.

Client Appreciation Events

Brian, Scott and Chris Moore at NYSE...2018

Scott Moore with GA Governor Nathan Deal

Scott and Carla Moore at The Helm

Scott with Trained Advisors ...2018

Succession Plan Appointees

Moore's Wealth Management

Success Team

M. Scott Moore

CHAPTER 12

ATTRACTING YOUR FIRST CLIENTS

Many advisors are so happy when a new client comes along that they forget to ask for referrals right away. They focus on the paperwork, approval process, and all of the details of getting the new accounts set up. However, once that new client walks out of the door after the initial appointment, you are unemployed again if you don't have another prospect to replace them. It's a costly error when advisors don't focus on gaining referrals. They may be uncomfortable asking for referrals, or they lack a process that feels good to them and their new clients.

It is imperative that you shift your mindset and anticipate collecting referrals. Once you have a system for creating a steady stream of new referrals, which I teach in my mentoring program, your business and income will increase. Having referrals also reduces your stress. You won't be worried about where your next client is coming from if you always cultivate a list of prospects.

My success is built on referrals. It's standard in our industry to ask new or current clients, "Who do you know?" Put on the spot, they can't think of any names or are afraid to expose their friends to a high-pressure sales environment. I used another approach to build my new independent agency, and it was so successful that we still use it today.

Respect

The best way to win referrals is to be respectful to each person you meet with, whether they become a client or not. No one enjoys feeling sold to, therefore conduct all your appointments in a way that educates people but does not pressure them. If people enjoy meeting with you, they will be more likely to refer you to their friends.

To make people comfortable right away, I say, "You know, not everyone is right for my services, or I'm not right for them. About one in five people I talk with don't need my help. They are already doing well with their investments and don't need to make any changes. However, they like having a review to ensure everything is working well for them. Other folks find that they want to make some tweaks to their investments and want my help. Let's see what we can discover for you."

Starting an appointment, or what we commonly refer to as a "discovery session," in this way helps people relax and trust you. You are giving them the respect to make their own decisions and signal that you are not going to push them into anything. I also explain my role as a fiduciary so that they know I am required to suggest only things in their best interest.

Near the end of our conversation, it's time to ask for referrals. I frame the request like this: "Bill, has our conversation today been helpful? Well, I'm so glad you think so because I've enjoyed it too. Who do you know from your neighborhood, church, or around town that is getting ready to retire, maybe sold their house recently, or God forbid, went through a challenging life event like losing a loved one or becoming a widow, and might want to review their options with me?"

By prompting them with examples of the kinds of people who are a good fit for my services, it's easier for them to come up with names. If you have a new client who came to you from a public seminar, invite them to attend your next event and bring a friend. Say something like this: "John and Sally, it was so great to meet both of you at the seminar last month. Did you enjoy the evening and the information? Well, I'm hosting another event next month, and I'd love for the two of you to come and have dinner on me. Bring a friend who is near retirement, or has just sold their house, or God forbid, recently lost their parent or spouse or inherited some property, who might be interested in the financial information you heard from me. Now, if your friends are uncomfortable coming out to an event like that, it's no problem. I can easily see them in the office during a casual one-on-one get together over a cup of coffee. Will it be okay if my office gives you a call in about a week to confirm if you can come and to get the names of any guests so that we can make sure we have enough food and seating for them?" Always develop questions that will elicit a positive response.

Notice that I always give people categories of potential referrals and get their permission to make a follow-up call. If someone doesn't want to give me a referral right away, I'll ask again at their annual review. Some clients want to make sure they enjoy working with you before providing referrals. Train yourself always to ask, even when clients have been with you for many years. Those long-term clients are often your best referral source. In my mentoring program, I cover this in more detail. Additionally, I discuss another very commonly missed opportunity to get referrals to local professionals who my clients use for other services. I can then call on those people to build a professional referral network.

Start Collecting Referrals Today

When I was preparing to leave my captive environment and open Moore's Wealth Management, I collected as many referrals as I could. However, I did not act on them until I was working for myself. I would tell people, "Hey, thanks so much for referring the Smiths to me. I want to let you know that I have a bit of a backlog now and might not get to them for three to six months, but I will let you know when I contact them."

Then, when I set an appointment with the referral, I'd call the original client to thank them and let them know I have an appointment set up with their friends. Finally, I'd always call once more to thank the original client after the appointment and let them know the results in a very confidential way. I'd say, "Thanks so much for introducing me to the Smiths. What a great couple. They are going to come on board with us, and I sure appreciate you connecting us." If the prospect did not become a client, I'd say, "Thanks so much for introducing me to the Smiths. They are doing fine now and don't need my help at the moment, but I really enjoyed meeting them, and we are going to stay in touch with each other."

It is always crucial to thank people who give referrals and to keep them abreast of how things went. Your appreciation shows that you respect and care about them and the people they referred to you. This communication process alone will help you get more referrals. When people know that their friends will be treated well and enjoy their conversation with you, they will continue to refer others.

Do Your Homework

As part of your transition, you'll be selecting your Field Marketing Organization (FMO). As soon as you have this selection completed, start training on their model for live seminars and possible college class presentations, so that once you are free of your captive environment, you are ready to begin offering workshops and classes. Polish your public speaking skills and practice the seminar or college class format from your new FMO, as it may be different from those used in your captive situation. Learn as much as you can about the products and vehicles you'll be offering so you can confidently share them in seminars, classes, and sales presentations. Preparation builds confidence.

You can also research your community. Before I opened my office in Gainesville, I'd already researched the zip codes where ideal clients lived, selected a mailing company, and had a mailer prepared. I visited several restaurants and chose one with a private room for my seminars, negotiated food prices, and had everything planned. Within three weeks of opening my office, I sent mailers and offered my first public seminar. Once I became established, I began adding college classes and client appreciation events to my array of offerings.

Don't Forget The Phone

When you open your new office, be sure to have someone there to answer the phones during business hours. When you answer your own office phone, people sense that you don't have enough money to have an assistant yet, which suggests instability or lack of success. I had my wife and son helping me, so I'd plan my office hours around times one of them could be on-site to answer the phones.

It's okay if you need to have your office open less than forty hours each week in the beginning. Perhaps your office opens at 9:00 a.m. to 3:00 p.m. four days a week, and you use the rest of the time to see clients in their homes. An abbreviated schedule would allow you to hire someone part-time until your cash flow supports a full-time employee or a second part-time person. Your goal should be to have your office open Monday through Friday from nine-to-five as soon as possible, but you can work with a shorter schedule for the first few months if you must.

Get Established on Social Media

Launch your website and social media presence as soon as you start seeing prospects in your new community. People will want to check you out, and if you lack a website, questions arise in their minds. You can begin with a basic site and expand it over time.

Social media is increasingly important too. You should have a profile on *LinkedIn* and a business page on *Facebook*. Many retirees use *Facebook,* and *LinkedIn* is the premier networking site for professionals. If you have time, and you wish to participate on *Twitter* or other social media sites, you may, but consider the websites and apps where your ideal clients engage with social media and ensure that you have a professional profile there.

However, many retirees still read the newspaper, especially the local publication. It is essential for you to develop a good relationship with your local paper. When I first came to Gainesville, I met with the staff of the local newspaper and started to run some small business-card sized ads. Then, whenever possible, I submitted press releases to highlight our growth. When our office opened, when my son earned his fiduciary license, or we added more space or advisors, I'd always write a press release. My FMO named me "Rookie of the Year" my first year, which was another opportunity to get positive press. The word spread around town that Moore's Wealth Management was a positive addition to the business community, and we were on the move and committed to growth. That's a marvelous message to send.

Newspaper advertising is a long-term growth strategy. However, it pays off. After about two years of consistent advertising in the

Gainesville paper, our firm had substantial name recognition in the community. I still use newspaper advertising regularly and recommend you do as well, especially if you are targeting current retirees.

Participate in The Community

As a newcomer, I needed to work hard to network with other professionals. I joined the Chamber of Commerce, the Rotary Club, and participated in as many events as possible. I accepted anytime anyone invited me to give presentations. I also made appointments to network with other professionals in complementary professions such as attorneys, CPAs, and Realtors.

Whether you are new to your community as I was, or you've lived there for years, opening your new agency requires that you invest time and effort networking with other professionals and supporting local businesses. You may think you don't have enough time to attend networking events or that the expense of hosting a "business after-hours" or other events is too high. However, when you invest time in earning the support and respect of other professionals in your community, you will discover new referral sources and great word-of-mouth recommendations.

Be Fully Committed

As you read this chapter, you may be worried that you won't have time to do everything it takes to grow your new business. It will be challenging at times, especially during the first years. However, the time invested in your first few years will pay off as your business and income grow. Remember that my personal income rose from an average of one hundred fifty thousand to five hundred seventy-five thousand dollars in my first year as an independent advisor. It was hard work, but the rewards for my family and me were life changing.

Failure was not an option, so I found the strength to work hard and do everything I could to make my first year successful. My wife and children blessed my efforts with incredible support. I fully committed to my success because I never wanted to return to the captive environment where my income and potential were limited.

You'll need the same commitment during your first year and the years to follow. However, now you are working for yourself, instead of a corporation, and the rewards benefit you directly. It will be well worth the effort you expend to become an owner instead of an employee.

CHAPTER 13

MARKETING AND EVENTS TO MAINTAIN YOUR GROWTH

Whether you are growing a brand new independent financial services firm or using the material in this book to revitalize your existing independent firm, you'll want to keep improving every year. Constant growth demonstrates that you are committed and doing the right thing for your clients and your community. That growth motivates you and your team, tells your family that their support and sacrifices were worth it, and shows your community that your firm is a safe place for their hard-earned money.

Your ultimate goal is to bring in new clients consistently and predictably, while also growing residual income every year. As you add more advisors to your team, you'll expand your capacity and your reach. Later in this book, you'll read about how to bring in more advisors. But first, let's concentrate on how to grow your client base and prospect list continually.

Marketing and Advertising

It will require twelve to twenty-four months of consistent advertising on social media and in your local newspaper (remember those retirees that still read the news) for people to recognize your name. Once that happens, change the focus of your marketing to highlight what you do. When we reached that point, we continued to post press releases about each new staff member or advisor who joined our team, office expansions, community events we sponsored, and any industry recognition we received. I kept a line item in the budget for ongoing advertising even though most press releases are free. We also advertise in a few small publications targeted to affluent neighborhoods or retirees.

Realize that retirees get many workshop and seminar invitations in the mail. If they are not familiar with your company, it is unlikely they will spend the time to attend your seminars or even read the invitations. Social media and newspaper advertising will build that familiarity.

After two years of advertising in the paper, I began to focus on educating people about what we do. In chapter 11, I explained how I wrote educational articles, called advertorials, which ran in the Sunday paper for several years. Some newspapers will charge you for those articles, while others will not. When I approached my local newspaper and offered to write a financial education column for free, I told them this would add value to their paper and assist readers, which it did. By covering a wide variety of financial topics, I got many positive comments from prospects and clients. People started to call for appointments after reading those advertorials, many times without even attending a seminar. For your legal protection, remember to have your compliance team approve each article.

We were approached about doing billboards or radio advertising but declined. Most retirees read their local paper daily, if for nothing else than to check the obituaries. Newspaper advertising was the most cost-effective way for us to reach our ideal clients. If you serve a different demographic, target your advertising to advertising media where you can reach your ideal clients effectively.

Consider heavy advertising/advertorials for at least the first five years of your business. That is a sufficient period to demonstrate stability and longevity. You can track your return on investment by asking people where they heard about you to ensure that your marketing dollars are working effectively. Today our business is 60% referral based so we can spend quite a bit less on advertising, but we continue to have a regular presence in local newspapers and on social media.

Give People Something to Talk About

Moore's Wealth Management has become famous for hosting fun community events. We started with the "50-Plus Dancing Diners", hosting monthly events for people over fifty, with a discounted dinner and dancing to a live band. Each dance was another opportunity to meet new people, show our support for the community, and send a positive press release to the newspaper.

Next, we added special appreciation events for our clients. For many years, we hosted a Senior Prom, which was a smashing success. We invited all our clients to an elegant dinner dance with a live band. Many of them had not attended a high school prom, so this event was extremely popular. We selected a theme each year, such as The Roaring Twenties, Fabulous Fifties, Phantom of the Opera, etc. Carla would work for months planning the menus, securing a band, flowers, decorations, and all the little touches that make the proms special.

At our prom, we'd crown a King and Queen, based on the people who gave us the most referrals that year. The winners received a sash, a cloak, and a crown. The newspaper would come to take photos and write articles about the events. Our entire team would be there, dressed in our best, enjoying the evening with our clients. It was amazing to see the competition build each year as to who would receive the crowns for referring the greatest number of potential clients.

After the first Senior Prom, people would ask about next year's theme, excited to learn the details. Clients brought their friends, and the events grew larger each year. A few years ago, a couple came up to me after the prom and said, "Scott, we want to tell you something. We are not one of your clients. We came with the Mitchells. We have never seen a happier group of people or anyone that cared more about people than you and your family. We want to be a client. I'm just telling you, we will come into the office, but we are telling you right now, we want to become a client." The proms were one of our most successful community events.

We recently had to stop hosting them because there was not a local venue large enough to hold all of our clients and their friends. Today, we offer two or three client appreciation events each year, and about 200-300 people attend each one. We've held picnics, tours of the botanical gardens and train trips in the mountains, to name just a few of our appreciation events.

You can use these ideas in your community. The goodwill and fun you provide will bring you more referrals and keep your current clients feeling like family. Whenever you can build your community and bring smiles to people's faces, you will reap a great return on your investment. Creating successful client appreciation events for your firm and covering all the details is part of our coaching/mentoring program.

Create a Client Advisory Board

Because we were continually growing and expanding, I was invited to participate in events for some of the top producers of various national insurance companies. At one such event, I met a man from Kansas City who told me about creating a client advisory board. He said that he wanted to have more clients, but only clients who were friendly, appreciative, and who he could enjoy serving. So, he asked his best clients to help advise him on how to attract more people similar to themselves. He told me, "Get those clients you like the most and that like you the most, ask them to rate your company on what you're doing right and wrong. It might be hard for them to talk about areas of improvement but suggest some examples where you believe you can improve and this will begin the communication."

I thought this was a terrific idea and implemented it as soon as possible. I invited ten of my best clients to be part of my Client Advisory Board, which meets over lunch every quarter. I called each one personally using this sort of a script:

Scott: *Hey John, this is Scott Moore. How are you doing? I've been thinking about this for a while, and I hope you guys know how highly I think of you and how much I care about you. I really enjoy being around you, and I hope you feel the same about us.*

John: *Oh, absolutely.*

Scott: *John, I want to ask if you would consider a favor. It's not much, but it means a lot to me. If you've got a couple of minutes, I would like to share an idea with you.*

John: *Well sure.*

Scott: *Listen, I've decided to put together a very select group of clients, probably no more than nine or ten that have done quite a bit for Moore's Wealth Management. People who have referred friends to us or who have given us great ideas. You and Sue are at the top of that list.*

Would you and Sue consider coming out to a lunch gathering to give us some feedback? We're going to be talking about the inner workings of our company. We'd like you to advise us on how we can do better and about anything we're doing wrong. We want to know because we want to attract more people just like you and Sue.

Now, we can't compensate you, as you know. The SEC won't allow us to do that, but we can buy you a nice lunch. We will have some nice gift bags, golf shirts, and you and Sue will get first invites to all of our client events, along with priority seating during our seminars. We'd be so honored if you would consider this.

Every person I asked said yes.

We hold the quarterly meetings in a nice restaurant in a private room. Carla and the staff decorate everything beautifully and create elegant gift bags for the attendees. We purchased beautiful leather binders with our logo embossed on the front for each person and made sure we treated everyone with honor and respect.

Each meeting has a specific, printed agenda. We review the minutes from the last meeting, results of the past quarter, upcoming events, and then ask for feedback and any areas where we could improve. At first, people only gave us positive feedback. That was helpful, but we needed more information on how we could improve. I'd have to come right out and ask them what was annoying or bothersome about interacting with our firm. I learned valuable lessons. Some were small, such as when our receptionist sounded busy or distracted when answering the phones. Other things were related to our seminars or discovery sessions.

This feedback was invaluable and helped us improve consistently. And the minutes taken at each meeting were sent to each member within a week. Then, we'd review each item and the corrective action taken at the following meeting so that people knew we were listening and responding to their suggestions.

In the first year after we started the Client Advisory Council, those initial ten members were responsible for one-third of all our company referrals.

Co-Marketing with Local Professionals

We joined the Chamber of Commerce in the counties where we serve a large number of clients, as well as in Gainesville. It's not been possible to attend every event or even be active in each organization, but it's important for our credibility to be a member of the local Chamber. Membership gave me speaking opportunities, the chance to sponsor events and to network with local professionals. When we did a significant expansion or remodeling of our office, the Chamber would come out for a ribbon-cutting ceremony.

I have not participated in other leads groups. For me, they are less effective than getting referrals from clients and professionals. Because I have significantly benefited from networking with other professionals who could be good referrals for some of my clients, I recommend you form positive relationships with:

- Attorneys
- CPAs
- Medicare Supplement Insurance agents
- Property and Casualty Insurance agents
- Realtors

When you approach these professionals, let them know that some of your clients may need a referral to their services. Get to know them and invite them to attend one of your seminars so that they can see what you do and feel comfortable referring appropriate people to you as well. One of the best compliments I've received was when one of our local CPA's sent his parents to me. They eventually became clients.

These professional referral arrangements take some time to develop but are immeasurably valuable. You get advertising you don't have to pay for and can confidently refer your clients to a trusted professional when they need help. It's essential that you give referrals as well as seek them. One of our attorneys told me that one year 75% of his business came from us. He is always glad to reciprocate. Our mentoring program offers a specific and detailed process for developing these professional relationships.

Embrace A Lack of Balance

All the techniques in this chapter will require time and effort but stack the deck in favor of your success. When you have the end in mind with the clear, concise mental picture (CCMP) of your success, you will be willing to devote the time and effort into building your financial services firm into a successful business.

I've always believed that you can't live an extraordinary life on an ordinary schedule. The first five years of your business, your life will be out of balance at times. You'll need to work more hours than you or your family might like. However, as you grow and add to your team, you will free up more of your time. Today, eleven years into my business, I sit in on only a few appointments. My advisors are well-trained and do a great job. I work on more of an administrative level and am preparing my team for my retirement. The time I invested early on was worth every minute, and yours will be too.

Note: There is not enough space in this book to cover my suggestions on how to present effective seminars and educational events. For a free white paper on the best way to create engaging seminars and educational events, go to www.ScottMooreConsulting.com.

CHAPTER 14

MANAGING IMPRESSIONS

When I was in my twenties and working as a computer engineer, a small technology company in New Orleans was my employer. The company experienced some rough times and laid off most of the computer programmers.

One day the owner told us that a potential customer was coming in to tour the office. These representatives of a national company were in negotiations with us for a huge contract. There was only one problem. Our second floor, where all the programmers used to work, looked like a ghost town. It was full of empty desks and computers, with just eight programmers remaining of the twenty employed before the layoff.

The owner did a brilliant thing. He had all of us go up to the programming floor and make it look busy. We turned on all the computers, put books and notebooks on the desks, added pens, coffee mugs, and paperwork, to make it look like a bustling office. The remaining programmers spread out with some empty desks between each of them. The owner scheduled the tour over the lunch hour, so it appeared that the empty desks belonged to employees who had just stepped out for lunch.

The company won the big contract, and I learned a valuable lesson. It is crucial to pay attention to every little detail, so prospects and clients have the best possible impression of you and your company. Whether you are just setting up your office or want to increase your profits, spending time and thought on your office environment will be beneficial.

Remember that few people desire to come in for appointments to discuss their finances. It's a chore for most people. Prospects are worried they are going to be ripped off or pressured into something harmful to their financial future. Most approach the meeting with healthy skepticism, and some will even feel defensive or angry. Your environment can help them feel welcomed and comfortable, which will begin to establish trust.

Start at Reception

Your reception area is the "first and lasting impression" of your office and sets the tone for all your client interactions. Be sure you have a comfortable and welcoming seating area. Don't use rigid office furniture or plastic chairs. Never have outdated magazines lying around. Consider investing in an attractive living room set with end tables, lamps, and an area rug. Subscribe to the local newspaper and a few magazines that retirees enjoy. Ensure those magazines and papers are current and in excellent condition. Place a nice candy bowl in the area and fill it with high-end chocolates. Make sure to refill the container daily. Imagine the difference between being offered a candy bowl with two pieces of cheap hard candy versus a full bowl of expensive chocolates. Have fresh flowers brought or ordered in weekly or biweekly. Little touches can send a big message.

In the beginning, I could not afford expensive furniture for the reception area, so I moved the living room furniture from our home to the office. When people arrive they "feel at home" and part of a family. Your office décor needs to take priority over your home, as the payoff is tremendous. As your income rises, you can furnish your home with the furniture of your choosing.

Train your receptionist to be very warm and welcoming. When people arrive, offer them a beverage. We provide coffee, tea, hot chocolate, bottled water, and a variety of soft drinks. My current receptionist used to work in a retirement home as a greeter and is terrific at relating to seniors. People love her, and she puts them at ease immediately.

I had a staff member once who tried too hard to be welcoming. When she greeted people, she seemed offended if they declined a beverage and pestered them until they had something to drink. She'd ask them three or four times. Her intention was good, but she went too far. It is always wise for you to listen to how your receptionist and other administrative staff interact with clients. Provide compliments on what is going well, as well as coaching on how to improve any problem areas. Your receptionist is often the first face of your company. Ensure that he or she has the skills and training to make that first impression welcoming, trustworthy, and professional.

If you have your office in a Regus Workspace, or other shared office settings, ensure that the reception area is comfortable and welcoming. Pay attention to how the receptionist greets people. We used Regus space for our first satellite office in Alpharetta, GA. (but not for our main office as I counseled against, earlier in the book) When we negotiated the lease, I made sure we could have a two-room office suite on the first floor (easier access for retirees), our own refrigerator for beverages, and that the reception area looked professional and welcoming. When people arrive for appointments, the shared receptionist calls my assistant who comes out to greet the people and walk them back to the advisor office where they are offered a beverage before the discovery session begins.

If at all possible, you should never be the one to greet your clients or prospects. If you do, that sends the message that your company is not large enough to have staff, which harms your credibility.

Setting Up the Meeting Area

I never like to meet with people across a desk. It feels cold and unfriendly. Instead, I have a small forty-two-inch round table in my office, along with three comfortable chairs. We conducted all meetings at this table until we could expand and add a conference room.

Before clients or prospects arrive, prepare all your paperwork and place it in front of the chair facing the door. It is important that your visitors do not face the door, a clock, or a window. If they do, they will become distracted. There should be an easy-to-read wall clock behind them and facing your chair so that you can keep track of time without looking at your watch. If your assistant needs to get your attention, he or she can do so quickly if you are facing the door.

Place framed family photos, any licenses or diplomas, and your current certificates from the Better Business Bureau on the walls. Ensure that all images and certificates are current. Pictures and documents demonstrate your family values and build trust.

If you use a conference room, prearrange it as well. I suggest you have six chairs at your conference room table. Ensure that they are comfortable and attractive. Prepare the room by having your paperwork neatly placed near a chair opposite the door. Pull out two chairs and angle them for easy access so that prospects immediately know where to sit. Again, they should both be facing you, their backs should be toward the door, with no distracting clocks or windows in their view.

Pay attention to the hallway as well. In our main office, we have framed family photos on one side of the hall, including a large picture of the Panama Canal. My grandfather helped to build the canal so that photo is a great conversation starter. We have pictures of all our ancestors who served in the military, plus wedding photos of both of our parents. Each photo highlights conservative family values, which appeal to our clients. The wall on the other side of the hallway is full of framed pictures from award ceremonies, my meeting with the governor, and framed newspaper and magazine articles that highlight the success of the firm. If you are using a shared office, you may not be able to decorate the hallway, but you can fill your offices with family photos and awards. Photos demonstrating tradition, stability, conservative values, and growth are appropriate. Adjust the images you select to appeal to your ideal client and community to ensure a good match. Instead of buying art prints, fill your walls with photos that demonstrate who you are and what you value.

Always Build Trust

It is up to you to develop and follow a sales process that ensures trust and educates prospects without making them feel pressured. You'll learn how to train your associate advisors in that process in later chapters. I've found that thorough preparation is essential. If I am unprepared, or unsure of the facts, I feel shaky, and prospects sense that discomfort.

Never rush. My sales process generally involves several meetings, especially if the prospect has an extensive portfolio. A multi-step process will ensure that you have plenty of time to build relationships.

Be sure to address people by name. Many advisors will inadvertently lose potential clients when they direct all of the conversations toward a husband and ignore the wife. When you work with couples, be sure to spend time building a relationship with both of them, asking each for questions and input, and using their names every three to five minutes. Don't assume that the husband makes the financial decisions.

We recently brought in a new client with a multi-million dollar portfolio. This gentleman attended several of our educational events and had his initial meeting at our satellite office. When he set up his second meeting, he was ready to bring in his wife and move his entire portfolio. He told Mark, the advisor working with him, that he'd visited a competing office and felt rushed, pressured, and did not enjoy the process. Our flow of educational events and initial meetings so impressed him that he was ready to make a decision right away.

Mark is a very seasoned professional and an excellent advisor. When he called me to share the good news, we strategized on the best way to ensure the meeting would go smoothly. The challenge was that Mark had not yet met the wife and would need time to build a relationship with her while processing a good deal of paperwork to move multiple investment accounts. The wife was attending the meeting in the middle of her workday and would have a limited amount of time.

We decided to move Isaac, one of our case preparation specialists, to that office for the day. Isaac would prepare all the documents and work with the husband on the data needed and on gathering all the signatures. Mark would then be free to build a relationship with the wife and answer any questions from the couple. Bringing another staff person to the satellite office was an easy way to streamline the process and free Mark to continue his work of educating and building trust.

Always look for ways to make things easy for your clients and your team of advisors. When you can remove any barriers to the sales process, everyone wins.

When A Prospect Is Not A Fit

You will have some prospect meetings that do not go well. It may be that the prospect is waiting to sell a property, finish a tax situation, is not a good fit for your agency, or your personalities don't mesh. Rather than pushing to fit a square peg into a round hole and frustrating everyone, have a process that will let you end meetings professionally and keep the door open to future work.

Thirty or forty minutes into a meeting that is not going well, I'll end the session. I close my presentation binder and say, "You know, I have certainly enjoyed our time together. Your time is valuable, and ours is too. I'm not seeing a good fit right now. Maybe we should pick this up at another time." I am careful to speak in a friendly and non-defensive tone. I say "our" time is valuable instead of "mine," to avoid giving offense. Then, I stand up. The prospect will stand too and prepare to leave. He or she may suggest another meeting when their situation changes. I escort them out and thank them for their time and the opportunity to get to know them better.

This kind, inoffensive approach leaves the prospects with a favorable impression of you and your agency. They may return to you in the future. At the very least, they won't have a sour feeling about your company. The last thing you want is unhappy people saying negative things about you in the community or on websites like *Yelp*. Dale Carnegie was right. In every interaction seek to "win friends and influence people." When you manage your environment skillfully, are well prepared, and do everything in your power to build a positive relationship, you are stacking the deck in your favor.

M. Scott Moore

CHAPTER 15

STAFFING YOUR OFFICE

We've already discussed the importance of employing a receptionist. Many new independent advisors will work with just a receptionist who also does filing and other administrative tasks for a good while. However, eventually, you will be operating at full capacity and need to bring on additional help. If your revenues have reached two-hundred fifty thousand to five hundred thousand dollars per year, you will start to feel stressed. When you become overwhelmed, my recommendation is that you bring in a technical person to be your Case Support Specialist (CSS), who can also handle client support for existing clients.

This role is ideal for someone with strong technical skills and already licensed in insurance. If they are not, they should be willing to become insurance licensed right away and then get their Series 65 Fiduciary license, as well. Or, if you have a recruit with excellent people skills who could become an associate advisor in the future, start him or her as a CSS first. This position is an outstanding place to learn the ins and outs of financial advising.

My son Chris was my first CSS and joined the agency at the very beginning. He had his insurance licenses and outstanding people skills. Becoming a CSS helped him learn and helped me serve more people. In time, I trained Chris as an associate advisor and brought my son Brian on as a CSS.

A CSS should excel in research and in developing case files after the initial appointment. It is a very detail-oriented job, so I created a checklist and several forms to make the task simple. After an initial meeting with a prospect, I complete a worksheet that summarizes the appropriate risk level for the prospect and the kind of case I want to present. That form goes to the CSS along with tax returns, statements, and other information collected during the initial meeting. Then, the CSS reviews the data, does research, and prepares a potential investment strategy to present at the second prospect meeting.

With my engineering background, it was natural for me to create a process and associated forms that made this work easy for a CSS to complete after initial training. Everything is designed to ensure standardization, which helps reduce errors. The second appointment is generally set three to seven days after the first discovery session, so the CSS has time to complete the work and prepare the presentation folder. We use a standard organizational procedure in putting the presentation folder together so that I can go through things very smoothly during meetings without having to search for paperwork.

Since the information in the case file is so crucial, I review it with my CSS each time to ensure that things are in the proper order and completed thoroughly. The CSS requires intense training and supervision, especially at the beginning. However, it is a great help to the busy advisor. Bringing on a CSS is the easiest way to free up more of your time from paperwork and research so you can complete more prospecting appointments. It also helps you assess if this new employee has the personality and skills to become a successful associate advisor in the future.

Plan to start your CSS at an annual salary of around forty thousand dollars with a bonus program. I also provide a one-hundred-dollar bonus for each case preparation that leads to a new client. If the CSS completes ten cases which convert into clients in a month, they receive an additional five-hundred-dollar bonus, bringing the bonus total to one thousand five hundred dollars. That kind of money is very motivating and paid only when you and your firm are making money.

After Chris completed training in his CSS role, I had him sit in on appointments. This helped him learn my sales process as well as introduced him to new clients. He learned to handle client support as well as serve as my backup for questions if I was out of the office or busy with new prospects. It was important that clients knew him and could associate a face with a name when contacting the office for support. He also attended all my seminars and public events. I wanted people to know and like him as much as they liked me.

Personal Characteristics Required

I tend to place people in two categories- those who excel in people skills and those who are more technical. Both can be effective in the CSS role. My son Chris is very skilled with people and wanted to become an associate advisor from the beginning. He was non-technical.

After a few years of growth in this position, I promoted Chris to Associate Advisor and brought my son Brian in as the new CSS. Brian, like me, is technically oriented and enjoys the research and technical work more than Chris. Brian implemented enhanced systems within our review process. Both of them learned well in their CSS roles, and both became successful advisors even though Brian had no previous sales experience. I followed the same training procedure with Brian that I had used with Chris. You can easily duplicate a successful system.

You can hire either a people person or a technician in this role. Each will require individual training to ensure their success. A people person will need careful training and supervision to ensure that all the technical details get handled correctly. A technical person will need training on how to participate in prospect meetings without overwhelming people with technical information or speaking taciturnly. Watch for natural strengths and train each recruit thoroughly so with time he can overcome any weakness.

Resistance

I imagine some of you feel that bringing on a CSS requires too much work on your part. I've trained many advisors and can affirm that there is a reluctance to bringing another person in on your sales calls, seminars, and presentations. And some advisors prefer to fly by the seat of their pants and don't want to be bound by written processes.

To grow an independent advisor firm and maintain the multi-million dollar revenue mark, you must overcome your personal resistance to documentation and staff training. It's impossible for one advisor to have enough time to secure and service the number of clients required for successful growth. If you attempt to do all things yourself, you will burn out in a few short years. The only way you can reach your long-term financial goals is to embrace the idea of building a well-trained team.

Your team is part of your office family and should participate in public events as often as possible. Introducing them to your clients and the community is a great way to demonstrate the stability of your agency. It also gives you the opportunity to praise team members in a public setting for their contributions to your success.

In my captive agency, I was pressured to build teams and found it stressful, especially when working with people on a part-time basis who were not fully committed to becoming financial advisors. I invested so much time and effort into helping others, yet very few became successful.

When I opened Moore's Wealth Management, I was determined to do things differently. I decided to build my team slowly, employing people that I trusted could succeed in the industry, and bringing a deep commitment on my part to be the master-copy. I learned to break down the things I did without thinking into lists of specific behaviors which build trust so I could teach them to my team.

Every employee you add must represent the same values and commitment to customer service that you have. The only way they can learn is if you teach them, and then monitor their performance so you can praise what they do well and correct any errors. Some advisors want to be nice and are reluctant to give staff feedback. This reluctance to addressing issues will cause many headaches and potentially a loss of clients. Build time into your schedule for regular meetings with your team members. Always point out what they do well and clearly show them how to improve any problematic behaviors. Address issues as soon as possible, so that little problems don't get out of hand.

Because new team members require the most significant investment of time and energy, stagger your hiring so that you get one person fully trained before you bring on someone else.

Hire Carefully

The majority of my team are family members, friends, or referrals from people I know and trust. I like to work through referrals rather than just putting advertisements in the newspaper or on social media. Our industry exposes people to sensitive information which must be kept private. It also requires high levels of professionalism, integrity, and people skills so clients and prospects feel comfortable. For these reasons, I am very selective about who I bring on my team.

My goal is to use three approaches for recruiting a new team member:

1. Endearment – getting people to like you and the workplace

2. Loyalty – earning loyalty by fair treatment and thoughtful training

3. Reward – providing ongoing praise, salary increases or bonuses, and other rewards which cement the desire to stay with the agency

Safely Endear Yourself to Staff and Clients

I've always believed in endearing people to me by introducing them to my family and inviting them to my home. It's essential to treat your team well, but not to cross the boundary where they forget you are their employer, and not just a friend or family member. Always document any performance issues and any steps taken to correct the behavior.

I also learned that any bonuses or rewards should link to the employee's professional conduct. For example, recently my current CSS, Isaac, has been working very hard and doing an excellent job during a busy time. He was getting ready to go on vacation, so, as a thank you for his extra effort, I had my administrative assistant give him two hundred dollars from petty cash before he left for his trip. On other occasions, I will give a hundred-dollar bill to an assistant who's done extraordinary work and tell him or her to go out to dinner with their spouse on me in appreciation for doing such a great job. When my advisors travel, I'll upgrade their airline ticket to first class if they have been demonstrating outstanding results.

I let the team know that we want to ensure our work environment is safe for everyone. As male advisors, we never see a single female client after hours without ensuring that there is another person in the office along with the male advisor, generally one of the female administrative staff. Should I have a female associate advisor, I would train her to never meet in a male client's home but to conduct meetings in our office or another public place. Both my staff and clients deserve protection from any uncomfortable situations.

If you feel unsure about your ability to hire and manage staff, consider working with a coach or taking some training courses in personnel management. Many advisors are new to staff hiring and supervision, so additional training in this area can be quite useful.

M. Scott Moore

CHAPTER 16

ATTRACTING GREAT ASSOCIATE ADVISORS

I'll admit it, when I left my captive agency, I was burned out and skeptical about recruiting others. You know the drill, we are trained and encouraged to recruit others so that we can get a portion of their business, and to get access to their contacts.

In my almost twenty years with that company, I recruited thousands of people. The focus there was on quantity rather than quality. Some of my recruits were successful and stayed in the industry, while many others quit when things got too hard, or they got a better opportunity. If someone was willing to start working, even on a part-time basis, I'd do everything I could to help them become successful. I'd invite people to my home, spend time on the weekends and during the evenings training them, and share my best tools and techniques for success. I knew I'd gone too far when one of my recruits called me at 3:00 a.m. and asked me to bail him out of jail.

Because of all that stress, drama, and wasted effort, when I started my independent agency, I had no plans to bring on other advisors. However, after watching me succeed as an independent advisor, my son Chris, who had been with me on the brokerage side of the business and was currently working as my Case Preparation Specialist, asked me to train him to be an advisor.

I thought about this carefully. Chris was my son, and I wanted to help him grow in his career. He'd been working with me for a while, and I could see his potential. However, if I could not train him to be successful as an advisor, I would damage our relationships in both my professional and my personal life. The risks were high. I knew that if I were to recruit and train Chris in the same manner I received training in my captive work, it could be a disaster on many levels. To do this right, I would have to create a training system for him that would be effective for everyone.

That system worked. Today I have three associate advisors and one in training who do a tremendous job. They represent the agency and me well, and I'm incredibly proud of them. They write the majority of the new business now and have made significant contributions to their own incomes, our agency's profits, as well as my personal income and quality of life. I am grateful to all of them.

I highly recommend that you consider recruiting and training a few associate advisors as well. You don't need a huge number. It is wiser to have a small number of highly trained associate advisors who have earned your trust and confidence, than a large group who you don't know well.

Because your name is on the door, you are entirely responsible for the behaviors of your associate advisors. If there is a problem with their work or ethics, you're the one held accountable. For that reason, your recruitment and training process must be slow, methodical, and structured.

Change Your Mindset

You and I may share the same background of pushing to recruit people quickly and finding ways to profit from them immediately, primarily from accessing their contacts. This mindset will not help you build a successful independent agency.

1. It is important to realize that when you train an associate advisor, they will not produce any income for your firm for nine to twelve months while they are in training. Thus, you need to have a substantial amount of business which can support you plus pay their base salary during training. I waited until my third successful year to bring on a new associate. During his training period, I was responsible for all the agency's production, so I had to work just as hard on selling and on attracting new clients as I had in the past.

To illustrate this point, let me share some numbers so you can see the contribution of my three associate advisors:

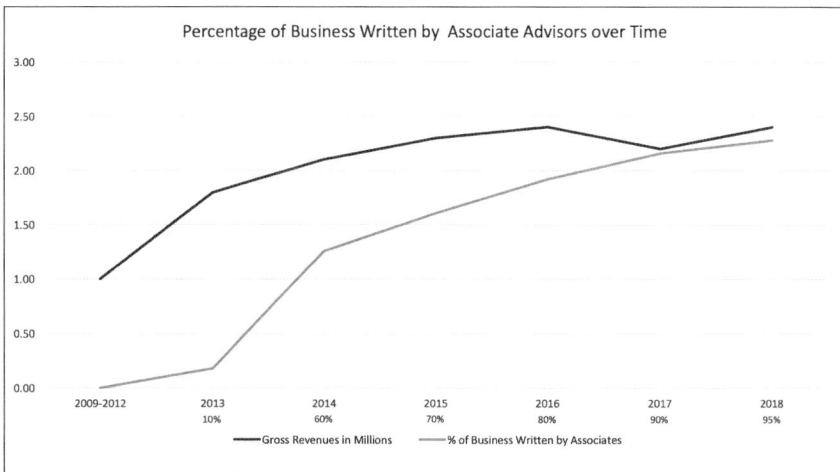

Percentage of Business Written by Associate Advisors over Time

- 2009-2012: I made all the sales, and our gross revenue was approximately $1 million by the end of 2012

- 2013: The three associates began to write some new business. Gross revenue rose to $1.2 million

- 2014: Gross revenue was at $1.5 million. I was writing about 40% of the new business while my associates wrote 60%

- 2015: Gross revenue rose to $2 million. I continued to reduce my levels of new business, writing 30% of the new business as the associate advisors increased theirs to 70%

- 2016: Gross revenue reached $2.2 million. Associates wrote 80% of new business

- 2017: Gross revenue was $2.3 million. Associates wrote 90% of new business

- 2018: Gross revenue was $2.4 million. Associates wrote 95% of new business

Today I don't write any new business at all. My three advisors are now fully trained, working as advisors without supervision, and I am now able to do more administrative and leadership tasks. Each of them has a distinct specialty in the agency so that prospects are assigned based on their needs instead of by which advisor is next in line for a prospect. The advisors work well together and are continuing my legacy of excellent customer service and strong ethics.

These numbers clearly illustrate the power of having a team of advisors instead of just one producer. It would not have been possible for me to reach these levels of revenue while working alone for any length of time. Additionally, note that I began to slowly withdraw from taking on new clients as my trained advisors became more proficient. This withdrawal helped them grow in confidence and financial reward. We all are sharing in the rewards of growing the agency to a higher level.

2. I never asked my advisors-in-training about their contacts. For one reason, my first two new advisors were my children, and the other was a good friend from my church. I did not recruit them for their contacts. Instead, I focused on training them so well that I could trust them with my prospects. This

is an important distinction. I selected my associates based on their skills, talents, and values, not who they knew, because I realized I could continue to use my systems for attracting quality prospects if I had trustworthy associates who could follow my sales process.

3. I never advertised when looking for an associate advisor. Instead, I carefully observed people I knew well. I watched for the proper values, work ethics, and abilities. Instead of trying to recruit a pool of qualified candidates and convincing them that working with me was a good plan, I chose recruits from among the people who met the parameters of the position. This process put me in the driver's seat so I could control the pace of recruitment and ensure that new associates would align with my style and values.

That approach was very successful. However, I did have requests I had to turn down from friends who wanted to work with me. Because I was quite clear on the characteristics required for success, I knew some of my friends would not be successful. It was kinder to decline than to offer them false hope and train them for work that would not suit them.

Keep Your Eye on The Prize

If it concerns you that adding associate advisors may be too hard and too much risk, let me remind you of the ultimate goal. For you to create a multi-million dollar financial services firm, you will need help. One advisor working alone cannot easily achieve those financial goals over any length of time. That level of success requires a well-trained team.

Your final mindset change is to think about recruiting as a long-term business growth strategy. You will build the organization and then bring in a few others who can help you take the organization further. Ideally, you'll include a plan to give them partial ownership in the future when you are ready to retire or move on. Your mindset should go beyond your career to focus on building a company that can serve your clients for the long term, even past your days of leading it. You are no longer building a career solely for yourself; you are creating a business that will endure, contributing positively to your community, your clients, and your residual income for many years.

Change Your Behavior

To bring in successful advisors and train them correctly, you must be willing to be transparent about your business practices and ready for others to observe everything you do. Some advisors hate to have others watch them do prospect calls or presentations. However, watching you is one of the best ways for your new advisors to learn, especially if you teach them both what and why you do certain things. Back in my broker days, we were told never to do a presentation alone. In some ways, that is a very wise adage. Always have someone sitting next to you learning how to do what you do. If you are presenting to clients by yourself, you are unemployed every day.

Once you bring in your first new advisor, you'll be teaching him your process. I suggest a combination of checklists and written documentation as well as many hours of observing you with clients and prospects. As he demonstrates understanding, you'll gradually be able to give him roles in seminars and appointments. Over time he will master each portion. You will be the master-copy for all of the technical and people skills required. That means that you're being watched all the time.

You don't have to be perfect to be a master-copy. It will be helpful for your advisors-in-training to see how you handle errors, prospects who are not a good fit, or communication during market downturns. You are human and will make mistakes. Your years of experience have taught you how to recover from mistakes, challenges, and setbacks. This information is invaluable for your new advisors.

I had to make one other very significant change in my behavior. I'm a driven, Type A personality. I like to move fast and can become impatient, especially with myself. When I was training my new advisors, I drove them crazy by asking:

- How's it going?
- How many appointments do you have set up?
- Who is coming in to see you this week?

I discovered these constant questions created frustration in my associate advisors. It concerned them that the agency might be having financial troubles because I seemed stressed over their production. That was the last message I wanted to send.

That experience taught me that I could be very aggressive with myself, but I had to be more patient with advisors who were still learning. I set up a weekly review meeting where we could discuss their progress, and I stopped badgering them in the hallway or at lunch. Since two of my advisors were my sons, keeping a healthy boundary between work and personal time was crucial.

If you are a hard-driving, high-producing advisor, you will need to learn patience with your new associates to accommodate for their learning. Developing this patience can be challenging. You may blow it at times and expect too much from people too quickly. If that occurs, apologize and move forward together. Tell your associates to let you know if you inadvertently ask them to do something they don't feel ready for or if you push them too quickly.

At the same time, there is a fine line between motivation, pressure, and enabling. Each of your new associate advisors will have a different comfort level and pace. To accommodate individual needs, I recommend you train just one new associate advisor at a time. Always stress the importance of open communication so you can give them honest feedback and they can do the same with you.

Your role as the master-copy will require you to give constant feedback to your trainee. Let your associates know this at the very beginning of your work together. Explain that you will be their coach and mentor, so you will continuously give them feedback designed to help them master the profession. You'll need to comment on what they are doing right as well as areas for improvement. Share your proposed training schedule so they understand that they'll be gradually taking over more and more tasks, but that it won't happen until they have learned each step in the process. When both of you can be patient, the process will be much more comfortable. But you, as the leader, will require the greatest patience.

How to Spot Solid Candidates

In 2009, shortly after I opened Moore's Wealth Management, I was sitting next to a man at a church event. I'd known him for many years. He'd been a leader in the congregation, had a stable family life, and a career with a solid history of growth and progress. I also knew he'd recently been downsized. I told him I had a great deal of respect for him and his professionalism, and that if he were ever interested in learning more about becoming a financial advisor, I'd be happy to talk with him about it. He thanked me but told me he'd started a new career in real estate and was pretty satisfied with it. Three years later he called me and went on to become my first non-family associate advisor. Like both my sons, he has become a top advisor in our industry.

Whether you are considering adding a family member or other person to your agency as an associate-in-training, it is vital that you carefully evaluate their values and behaviors. As you know, this industry is not for everyone. It is too much work to train someone who lacks the character, skills, and aptitude; so avoid heartache and carefully screen each candidate.

First, look at their work history. Does it show a pattern of job hopping or stability? Can you see evidence of growth and advancement? Look for stability as well as a personal drive to advance. If you see evidence of a willingness to learn new things and take on new challenges, this candidate may possess the ambition required to work in a commission-based industry like ours.

Evaluate their work ethic. Seek people willing to work hard, be a self-starter, and complete tasks independently. Someone who has successfully managed a team or worked themselves through school should have the drive and work ethic needed in our industry.

Both men and women make excellent financial advisors. At this point, I have only male associate advisors in my agency, not by design, but because those candidates best matched my needs. Due to our continued growth, my daughter Michelle, who minored in finance and worked for nearly four years in an advisor support role for a large company, is now joining the firm, and I am delighted. Many female advisors have greater success than males in many areas, especially when working with widows or single women.

Is the potential advisor open to seeking more education? Our industry requires certification and licensing exams, as well as the ability to understand various financial products and investments. Seek associates who enjoy learning and are willing to study for and pass examinations.

I also suggest selecting candidates with some leadership experience, either in a professional or volunteer setting. When people have been in a top position, they have experience in communication, relationship building, and achieving goals. These skills are very valuable in our profession.

In this industry, you can have great people skills and learn the technical side of things or exhibit excellent technical skills and learn to work well with people. Most people rarely are talented in both areas. My son Chris is terrific with people but does not enjoy detail work on the technical side. He was willing to learn the technical side and work against his strengths. My son Brian is the opposite. Detail work and technical issues come quickly for him. He worked hard to master the selling and people skills. Both of these young men are now highly successful advisors and principals in the firm. They have learned to maximize their strengths and learned skills in the other area.

Consider which areas you enjoy teaching. If you love the technical, detail work of our profession, you may want to bring on associates gifted with people skills so you can train them from your area of strength. If you shine with people, aim for those who are more technically inclined. I am fortunate to be equally comfortable with both technical and people skills so I can train any associate advisor. As you develop your team over time, you will want to build a balance of advisors with natural talents in both areas, just as a football team recruits for both offense and defense. My recommendation is that your initial associate is someone you can train from your area of strength.

The final areas to assess are values and ethics. This area is difficult to assess in people you don't know, which is why I like to recruit from people I know well. I look for honesty, personal responsibility, a robust ethical code, and stability at home. Our profession is demanding and stressful at times. If you bring on an associate advisor who has a lot of drama in his or her personal life, it will be difficult for them to focus appropriately on career mastery.

Remember that you will be introducing this person to your clients and prospects. Do they have the professionalism, character, and stability to represent you and your business positively? Do they inspire trust? Does their behavior and reputation in the community send a positive message?

Always remember that you are handling people's life savings. Clients and prospects trust you with their hard-earned money and believe you will manage it wisely and ethically so that they have funds for their golden years and for their heirs. The local bad boy or party girl will not engender the trust required.

M. Scott Moore

CHAPTER 17

TRAINING, COMPENSATING, AND SUPERVISING ASSOCIATE ADVISORS

There are two pathways for training successful associate advisors. I've used both and will present them here for your consideration, along with my recommended best practice. The paths are:

1. Entering as a Case Support Specialist with a base salary plus commission with a gradual progression to an advisor position, with a graduated percentage of revenues based on work completed.

2. Entering as an Advisor-in-Training without any compensation, to earn a more substantial commission in the future.

My first two associates, Chris and Brian, were young and benefited from pathway number one. Mark, my third associate, was in his fifties, had a long, successful prior career, and had the financial resources to invest six months at no salary in return for a quicker training period leading to rapidly receiving larger commissions. Since each individual has unique needs, you can determine the best pathway for your associates. My recommendation is that you use the first pathway as your primary tool. It ensures the best quality of life for your trainees during the process, especially if they are younger and still have the emotional and financial demands of a young and growing family.

The Case Support Specialist Pathway

Your new trainee will spend anywhere from twelve to twenty-four months in a case preparation role, mastering the technical side of the business. Using forms and checklists you create, they will complete research for prospects, prepare proposals based on appropriate risk levels, prepare reports for annual reviews, and later, complete some basic transactions with established clients. This approach gives trainees the opportunity to learn all of your products and services, to create potential portfolios and strategies, and gain some customer service experience with established clients.

The trainee can also begin studying for their Insurance and Series 65 Fiduciary licenses and attend your seminars and public events. You will introduce them to current clients, explain their role, and begin to build a positive relationship between them and your clients. These introductions are important for two reasons. First, to demonstrate that your business is growing and thriving. Secondly, to build the perception that your clients have a trusted team working with them.

Pay your Case Support Specialist a base salary of around forty thousand dollars with a performance bonus. As I explained in chapter 15, I provide a one-hundred-dollar monthly bonus for each case they prepared that results in a new client. If ten or more become new clients in one month, I add a five-hundred-dollar bonus on top of the hundred dollars for each new client. These financial incentives motivate and encourage precise work.

This initial period sets the stage for the remainder of the training. You want to instill professionalism, structure, and attention to detail. Because you have already designed your training process and the required checklists and forms, the CSS should be able to work independently on case preparation reasonably soon.

You will need to provide a high level of supervised instruction at the beginning, gradually decreasing it until you trust that your trainee can consistently do all the required tasks. However, it is always wise for you to review the case folders before each prospect meeting to ensure that there are no unpleasant surprises in front of prospects.

Advisor Training Transition

Phase One – Months one through three: After nine to twelve months in the CSS support role, your trainee will move to a dual role. They will train and supervise a new case preparation specialist and shadow you on all your appointments. During this shadowing, their only function is to observe, take notes, and stay quiet unless you ask them for input.

Note-taking is essential in all appointments. First, it forces the trainee to pay attention and listen carefully for pertinent details. Second, it shows your prospects and clients that the trainee is serious about learning, which builds their credibility.

After each shadowing session, dissect the appointment with your trainee so that they understand why you handled things in specific ways. They will be learning how to build rapport, sell, and present the technical aspects, so guide the discussion to ensure they caught all the lessons in each interaction. It is also imperative that you discuss areas that need improvement as well as areas where they performed well.

Phase Two – Months four to six: You train the new associate to present a small section of the first appointment. As they become proficient in one section, give them additional parts. They will first practice presenting that material to you so that you don't have to worry about problems with your prospects. Let them know that if you see any issues arise during a prospect meeting, you will jump in to help them. As you transition more portions of the meeting to your trainee, you will switch roles to become the listener and notetaker during the sections where you observe their work. By the end of this phase, the trainee should be able to lead all of the first prospect meetings with your observation.

Phase Three – Months seven to twelve: Train the associate to do portions of the second appointment, increasing their responsibilities until they can independently conduct first, second, and possibly third prospect meetings.

Phase Four – Second or third year of training: Begin to weave your new associate into your public seminars and college classes. Start with having him introduce you at the events. Over time, he will take over more of the presentations until he can present the full program comfortably and confidently. You will provide coaching and support for his prospect meetings, sitting in on them as your schedule allows, and debriefing with the trainee. You will assist in all meetings with high net worth prospects or those with complicated situations.

Phase Five – Year three or four: Your trainee is now fully independent in the role of advisor. You begin to enjoy the rewards of seeing more clients benefit from your services, as well as generating a financial override on the associate's business. You can continue to educate your associate on more of the administrative details of the business, especially if you have a succession plan which may lead to potential firm ownership in the future.

Compensate your new associate advisor with a forty to fifty-thousand-dollar base salary, including annual evaluations and salary increases, along with a 25-30% commission/fee share. As he grows in skill and can close more business, his commission and fee share will grow significantly with his more extensive client base. If he personally secures a big client without marketing assistance from the firm, you may want to bump up that commission to 35-40% for that case. Additionally, provide group health, dental, and vision insurance, along with a 401(k) plan. The business should contribute 50-65% of all the group insurance premiums for the advisor.

The Advisor-In-Training Pathway

For the few select candidates willing to work hard and train more rapidly without a salary, start them at Phase One of the Advisor Training. Compress the training so they are ready to manage prospect meetings and presentations within six to nine months. Their compensation should then be approximately 50% for all commission/fees. If they bring in a high net worth client, you can bump that commission to 55-60% for that client only.

Mark took this option. He immediately obtained all of his licenses and then shadowed me every day for six months, asking questions and soaking up information. After that, he was able to conduct parts of meetings and presentations. He moved through all the phases in the training plan, but at a more rapid pace because he'd had a long business career already and had solid people skills and sales experience.

Advisor Retention

Because I am careful about who I recruit as associate advisors, I do not require a non-compete agreement at that stage of employment. Most are difficult to enforce anyway. In my experience, it is better to invest in the team so that they want to invest in you. Loyalty builds when both sides contribute to the success of the firm. It is also important to continually talk about opportunities for advancement. If you have a future ownership plan, and I strongly suggest you create one, review that incentive regularly with your associates, including the vesting process. Once possible ownership options arise for them, a strong non-compete agreement should be part of your buy/sell options to cover any scenario in which they might leave the firm.

Supervision and Management

From the first day of training, communicate that you want your associates to succeed. Reinforce the vision of their future compensation and the potential for growth. Feed that vision with your continual feedback so that they can achieve their goals, and the business can thrive.

Remember, you are their teacher and mentor. The last thing you want to hear after an observation is, "Wow, you are awesome. I could never present that well." Their observation time isn't to get them to praise you, but to learn from you. Be humble and candid, sharing what went well and where you could have done things differently. Teach the subtle skills, such as reading body language, as well as the more obvious skills. While a compliment for your skills may be pleasant to hear, it does not help increase their confidence. You want them to see that what you do is simple and repetitive and that anyone can learn it.

One crucial skill to teach is that of building each other up in public. Show trainees how to compliment and thank you during meetings and appointments while you do the same for them. Explain that these compliments are not to boost your ego, but to demonstrate to prospects and clients that you are a team and fully support each other. Instruct trainees that any disagreements between the two of you should be reserved for your private meetings, never in front of clients or prospects. Presenting a united front in this way builds client trust.

Presenting feedback can be challenging for some mentor advisors who want to stay positive and not hurt anyone's feelings. That mindset will cause all sorts of problems. As I mentioned earlier, to be an effective teacher and mentor you will need to highlight both areas of strength and needed improvements. I use the Oreo method, sandwiching needed improvements between two strengths, just like the filling in a cookie. This approach reduces defensiveness in the trainee and helps you stay balanced in your feedback.

Providing feedback immediately after every interaction is not only key to your trainee's growth, but also wise. When your trainee begins to assist in public presentations, watch the videos together so that you can assess presentation skills. You may have some trainees who fear public speaking. Consider Toastmasters, Dale Carnegie, or other presentation training for additional skill development.

Be ready to recommend appropriate books or audio courses to help trainees. I always recommend Dale Carnegie's *How to Win Friends and Influence People* and Napoleon Hill's *Think and Grow Rich*. Though written years ago, the information in these books remains evergreen. Your FMO or RIA may also offer training and development courses for newer advisors. While you are the master-copy, weave in other training and personal development resources as needed to support individual training needs.

There may be times your trainees grow impatient to take on more responsibilities before you think they are ready. For example, they may feel prepared to tackle a prospect initial or closing meeting without you in the room. My suggestion is that you let them try, even if you believe they may face challenges. After about twenty minutes, go into the meeting, say hello and that you just wanted to stop by and see how things are going. You'll be able to tell if the meeting is going well and that it's only necessary to observe, or that there is a problem you need to fix.

At other times, your trainees may come up with an excellent idea, and you let them run with it. Mark, my third associate, developed the concept of presenting educational seminars at colleges and universities. When he introduced the idea, he felt he could research the materials on his own. Mark had prior experience in this area, so I trusted him to conceive and design those presentations. Both he and I, and now he and Chris, present these classes. He's done a terrific job and brought in many new clients from these programs. Another example entitled "Lunch and Learn" came from my son Brian. To assist Isaac, our CSS, with his advisor training and expand options for discovering quality prospects, Brian and Isaac are now hosting these presentations on a regular basis.

Your role as the master-copy never ends. I still randomly sit in on appointments and presentations, even though my associate advisors are working independently. I like to make sure no one is developing bad habits or drifting away from our established processes. You are always the leader of your business, so these periodic observations are important for a couple of reasons. They are opportunities to provide feedback and praise to your associates. Plus, you will be confident that clients and prospects are receiving the high level of service and professionalism you designed.

When to Repeat The Process

When your first trainee exits the Case Support Specialist position, bring in a new potential advisor to fill that role. Then, monitor the progress of both employees. When you feel that both have reached a level of mastery in their respective positions, you can begin the process of transitioning the trainee CSS into an advisor-in-training position and replacing him with a new CSS. This process may require one to three years. There is no rush. It is better to ensure that each new associate advisor has reached mastery before you shift your focus to a new associate.

Depending on your goals and long-range plans, a group of three or four well-trained associate advisors should be sufficient. I've grown my business to the multi-million dollar level with three additional advisors, carefully trained and coached by me. I'm proud of each of them and confident they will successfully carry Moore's Wealth Management well into the future.

M. Scott Moore

CHAPTER 18

SPECIAL CONSIDERATIONS WHEN WORKING WITH FAMILY MEMBERS

A few years into Moore's Wealth Management, family tensions arose. Three of my sons, Chris, Brian, and Kyle, were working full-time with me. Carla was doing a lot of work in the office planning events and marketing, alongside our daughter Michelle, who at that time worked on a part-time basis. My son Jonathan also helped with many client appreciation events. There were lots of Moores in the office.

One of my sons is very much like me, and our strong-willed personalities would clash at times. The kids would sometimes go to their mom with complaints about me or each other, and I still saw them as my children, not my colleagues at work. Non-family employees also at times felt caught in the crosshairs, and some were concerned about perceived favoritism or the tension in the office.

I realized I was driving everyone nuts because I talked about work all the time, even at family dinners. Occasionally my sons took advantage of the fact that I was the grandfather of their children. They didn't hesitate to take a day off or come in late when one of their children needed something, thinking I would be more understanding than the employer of their spouses. I could tell that my dream of a successful business that could also support my children and their families was about to end. There was a choice. We could stop working together, and I could return to working as a solo producer, or I could ask for help. I chose to ask for help and hired a consultant and his team who specialize in helping family businesses. It was a substantial investment but worth every penny.

The consultant and his assistant looked over all the particulars of our business and then spent two days in the office observing our interactions. On the third day we all, family members and other staff, sat down with them for a debriefing. First, the consultant went over some general observations.

Then he said, "Okay now, Chris, Brian, and Kyle. I want to talk to you for a minute." He turned to me and told me to stay out of the discussion. He continued, "Listen, from 8:00 to 5:00 p.m., your dad is trying to do nothing more every day than keep his clients from other advisors who want to take them away. He's also trying to win clients from other advisors. It's a constant battle. Your dad focuses on that battle all day long because he has to be successful. If he is not successful, you won't be either."

He then went on to tell them that from 8:00 a.m. to 5:00 p.m., the focus had to be on business, not family matters, unless it was a life-threatening situation. He preached the importance of total focus on business, not personal issues during the workday. I sat back and gloated a bit. Finally, someone was affirming what I'd been saying.

Then, he turned to me, asked the others to stay silent and said, "Dad, from 8:00 to 5:00, this is 100% business. We've already identified this, and they've agreed to do that. After 5 o'clock, it's not business anymore, unless you're doing a seminar together at night. When you go out to dinner, have them over to your house, or visit them, not one word about your business. Not one." I stopped gloating. He went on to tell me how important it was to separate family and work time and to eliminate my bad habit of making every conversation about work.

That moment and several others like it changed our business, our relationships, and our future. The family gained a new respect for me and how hard I worked to provide for them. I gained a new respect for them as adults who contributed to my success and outside of office hours, deserved time off with their dad, not their boss.

Since then, we have done a much better job of respecting each other and separating work and family time. We're not perfect, but things are healthier. It was vital that we had the help of the consultant who could come in, see our patterns, and talk frankly with us about what needed to change if we were to continue together. Improving our working relationships was particularly important when I brought in Mark, a non-family associate advisor who had a long history of professional experience. That situation could have created a lot of jealousy and mistrust on the team, but it didn't because we'd dealt with our family challenges already.

Pros and Cons of Working With Your Children

One of the best benefits of working side-by-side with your children, other than the obvious one of seeing them succeed, is the message it sends your clients. They see that your agency will continue safely managing their money even if you retire, become ill or disabled. The stability of having a team of younger advisors working with older advisors provides clients with great comfort, especially when all the advisors are Series 65 fiduciary advisors. Clients don't have to worry about moving their funds if their current advisor experiences a car accident or unexpected illness. I pay attention when prospects are considering our firm versus another independent firm with a solo advisor, or even multiple advisors, that have no internal succession plan. Although other firms might offer similar solutions, about 25% of those prospects tell me they chose us precisely because of the stability of the business, and our internal succession plan.

The second benefit is for you. Having your children work with you provides faith and confidence that the business you worked so hard to build won't disappear when you exit. When you've spent time and effort training and investing in your children, you can trust they will continue your work. The clients you so enjoy serving, the reputation you established, and all the processes you created will remain after you leave the business. Your income will continue as well, depending on how you structure your succession plan.

Finally, you can trust your children to be honest and ethical with you, clients, and each other, especially if you raised them well. I credit Carla tremendously, as well as our church family, for instilling strong values and ethics in all of our children.

However, there are challenges when working with family members. You all have a history together. Everyone remembers the big family fights, the mistakes children made as teens, and the mistakes parents made in the heat of the moment. It can be challenging to move past any hard feelings about the past and look at each other as adult colleagues.

It is also a challenge to train an adult child in the workplace. At times I found it hard to act as a mentor, instead of a parent. It was frustrating for the guys to accept feedback and instruction from me and not perceive it as a father's frustration or criticism, instead of input from a trainer.

I addressed these challenges by doing my best to reaffirm the benefits package for them whenever I could. If there was a question about compensation, I tried to be as generous as possible. I also reminded myself that they needed praise and acknowledgment as well as corrective feedback. I did not assume they needed less support from me than did my non-family staff just because my sons loved me as their father. It was essential to respect them while modeling the way to conduct professional relationships. I cover much more of this in my mentor and coaching program.

Building Trust with Clients

We used a long-range plan to introduce my sons to clients so trust would grow over time. This process works well for family members as well as any new associate advisors. First, I would introduce Chris or Brian at the client's annual review and praise him to the client for the work he did on preparing the review. The following year, Chris or Brian would conduct the meeting while I observed and continued to complement his work. By the third year, clients had developed confidence in Chris and Brian, so they handled annual reviews without me.

The entire office, family and non-family alike, attended our dances and client appreciation events. Clients and prospects became accustomed to seeing everyone and relationships began to develop. I trained everyone on proper etiquette for those events. It might be a party night for attendees, but it was work for us, a time to demonstrate professional and respectful behavior. Everyone knew the evening was a marketing event, not a party where they could let their hair down. Each of the staff had a specific well-rehearsed role and performed admirably.

We also used the multi-step training method you learned about in the previous chapter for seminars and events, as well as prospect meetings. The guys took on additional parts of each presentation until they could do it without me. Over time, clients were comfortable seeing any of the advisors in the firm, not just me.

Once all the associate advisors, my sons, and Mark, were independent and proficient in all aspects of their roles, we began to specialize. Each advisor had a specific specialty so that the advisor assigned to a new prospect had skills that matched their needs. We also divided up training responsibilities to align with those specialties. We built a team with distinct roles.

This division of labor was beneficial for prospecting as well. When someone visits our website or attends a seminar or college class, they immediately know which advisor is best suited to their needs. It also demonstrates the breadth and depth of knowledge on our team, sending a message that we can help a wide variety of people. Assigning each of the associates a role they thrive in helped to eliminate jealousy, competition, or overshadowing. Everyone has a distinct place to shine. Also, as each advisor acquires more experience, he soon becomes proficient at all levels, which is what our team looks like now.

Cheerleading

One of my sons sometimes has a sarcastic sense of humor (and probably gets that from me). Once or twice when he was first training with me, he'd make digs about me in a client or prospect meeting. I had to pull him aside and teach him the importance of presenting a harmonious, unified teamwork approach in prospect/client interactions. He meant nothing by it and did not realize the sarcastic comments were harming trust. He was trying to build a good relationship with the clients based on humor. I had to learn to refrain from sharing anything negative about their childhood, even in jest, when a client would say something similar about their children. Though both intents were good and just an attempt to bring some humor to the conversation, there is no place for this,

I teach all my staff, from receptionists to fellow advisors about the value of complimenting each other in public, not just to stroke their egos, but to show clients and prospects we all believe in each other. I cheerlead for my team, and they do the same for me.

Building up your associates, especially when they are your children, demonstrates your respect for them, as well as proof of your leadership. At the end of the day, you as the owner are responsible for providing a harmonious staff who communicates well and works together effectively. When clients and prospects observe those positive working relationships, trust in your leadership and the stability of the business grows. No one wants to place their money with an agency full of people who fight and bicker.

Indeed, there will be disagreements and tensions. Those challenges are typical in any work setting. However, by your leadership and training, you can teach your team to keep those disagreements behind closed doors, resolve them quickly, and return to providing exceptional service to your clients. As the master-copy, you must consistently model this behavior as much as you teach it.

M. Scott Moore

CHAPTER 19

BARRIERS TO SUCCESS IN THE MULTI-ADVISOR MODEL

Many of you reading this book are also trying to determine if moving into a multi-advisor scenario will be a good fit. I understand. The business model presented in this book is exciting. It offers great potential for financial success and personal fulfillment. It is also a lot of work and not for everyone. If you embrace it, you will recruit a few additional advisors, but most likely in a very different way than you do now.

In this chapter, you'll learn what it takes to succeed as the founder of a multi-advisor financial firm by looking at the characteristics of people who will not be able to make this model work. This information will be helpful as you evaluate yourself, and in the future, identify potential candidates to join your firm. It's important to know that I am not judgmental or disrespectful of the skills and qualities you have developed in your career. I am merely helping you examine your strengths and weaknesses, just as we assess the portfolios of our clients.

To create a firm that lasts, you need to be a leader, the master-copy for all of the advisors who work for you. As you review this material, take an honest look at yourself and see if you match the profile of a successful leader. If you do not, my recommendation is that you remain where you are, either in a captive position or working independently in a small agency, at least until you learn the skills of a leader or can be mentored by someone to help you. You can create a satisfying career in a traditional setting. However, if you dream of more freedom, personal income, and security for your family, the characteristics detailed in this chapter will be detrimental to your success.

Barrier 1: Lack of Integrity or Strong Character

When I was new to financial services, I went on a sales call at the home of a married couple I'll call Joe and Mary Smith, who were interested in a life insurance policy for Joe. When I arrived, Mary told me Joe was in bed with a terrible stomach flu and was probably contagious. We discussed all the options and Mary selected a policy for Joe, took the paperwork into the bedroom for his signature, and gave me a check.

A few weeks later, while waiting for the policy to be accepted, I learned that Joe was in prison for embezzlement. Mary duped me, knowing it is impossible to insure someone who is currently incarcerated. I immediately canceled the underwriting of the policy to ensure it was never issued.

The financial services industry continually challenges the advisors' character and integrity. There will be potential clients who try to mislead you, as well as many opportunities to take shortcuts or build in additional compensation that will be almost impossible to detect.

Even if you merely take shortcuts or do small things to get more money from clients, you will know that you lack integrity. That knowledge will eat at you and impair your ability to succeed. In the world of scammers, Ponzi schemes, and media reports of financial chicanery, both prospects and advisors fear being ripped off. If there is even one hint that you are not completely honest and committed to the highest level of integrity, your firm's reputation will be ruined, and your reputation will most likely never recover.

As you grow your multi-advisor firm, temptations will come at you from every angle. A staff member may try to begin a love affair, a new advisor may promise more than can be delivered, or another business owner may want information on your high net worth clients. At those decisive moments, the only thing you can rely on is your character.

Character reveals itself in every interaction. Consider these scenarios:

- When someone asks a question, do you pretend to know the answer or admit that you don't know and offer to find the solution and get back to them?
- When the market is falling, do you avoid answering your phone in hopes that it will recover the next day or week or month?
- When your cash flow is tight, do you borrow a bit from a client fund just for a few days? That is a serious violation that normally results in legal liability, loss of licensing, and even prison time. Benjamin Franklin said, "It takes many good deeds to build a good reputation and only one bad one to lose it."

Are you willing to commit to a lifetime of doing the right thing? In my mentoring program, I cover exactly how to structure your firm legally so that even the perception of mixing client funds with your own is impossible. Remember that a big part of overcoming objections with prospects is to cover them BEFORE the prospect raises them.

Barrier 2: Lack of An Incredible Work Ethic

My hobby is cars. I love restoring classic cars, attending races, and learning everything I can about engines. Engines are built at various sizes, depending on how much power the vehicle requires.

It is possible to take a small engine and overbuild it to produce more power. But that engine will never be as strong, or last as long, as a larger one with more cubic inches. In racing circles, we used to say, "There's no substitute for cubic inches."

Likewise, there is no substitute for a strong work ethic in financial services. To build your agency, you must be willing to work incredibly hard. I used to say, "I might not be the smartest person in the room or the one with the most advantages in life, but I can outwork just about anyone." If I had to point to the most significant contribution to my success, it would undoubtedly be my work ethic.

Because my father died when I was very young, money was tight for my family. From the time I was eight years old, selling newspapers to help my mother, I always had a job, sometimes a couple of them at the same time. Carla and I married when we were quite young and went on to have a large family. I had no choice but to work hard, and it paid off with the success I enjoy today. I was not an overnight success, and you probably won't be either.

When you are building a company, you will not be able to work nine-to-five and then go home. Most weeks will require evening and weekend work. Client acquisition, preparation, paperwork, planning, and ensuring that your clients know you are protecting their hard-earned retirement money demands a tremendous amount of time. It will call for an extraordinary commitment of your energy and effort during the first few years.

When I started my firm, I chose a locale in Georgia where I had no ties. In this town, people are a bit suspicious of strangers, especially those who move in and want to handle people's money. I had to work hard to prove I was trustworthy.

Sometimes I stayed at the office working so late at night that I'd sleep there in a sleeping bag. On more than one occasion the police tapped on the window at three in the morning and asked what I was doing. They did not believe a financial advisor would be in his office at that time of night, so I had to prove I was legitimate.

It was possible for me to apply myself like that only because Carla believed in me and handled everything at home. Without her support, I would not have the success I enjoy today. If you are considering opening your agency, first discuss the demands with your family and get their buy-in before you begin. Your work ethic may be powerful, but if your spouse or children are not supportive, it will be almost impossible to maintain your momentum.

In my nineteen years of recruiting potential agents for insurance and financial services as a captive employee, I worked with over one thousand recruits. Over time, I could quickly spot patterns in a resume that would alert me to an undesirable work ethic. Consider these signs of a potential problem:

- Job hopping: Avoid recruits with many different jobs on their resume

- Part-time employment: Many people try the financial services industry on a part-time basis while working elsewhere. I did this at the beginning of my career. However, when selecting agents for your multi advisor firm, steer clear of those unable to commit to working on a full-time basis. You will choose only a few associate advisors and want only the best. If your clients glean a whiff of instability in your firm, they will not trust you with their funds. A part-time advisor does not suggest the professionalism or dedication required to build and keep trust.

- Lack of initiative: It is possible to quickly go bankrupt in this industry if you are not a self-starter. You won't have someone looking over your shoulder to make sure you do what is required or that you use your time effectively. That kind of freedom is appealing to some but very difficult for others. To be your own boss, you must set the example and work harder than anyone else in your agency. Are you willing to do that?

Barrier 3: Failure to Put Your Client First

I knew a financial advisor extremely motivated by public recognition. He did everything he could to win awards and gain accolades. At times he sold his clients products that were not in their best interests so he could meet sales quotas and win contests. He was churning and burning to sell as many products as he could, without considering the long-term benefit to his client. Sometimes advisors get a financial incentive to push certain investment vehicles over others. Putting yourself first can be a slippery slope.

As a financial advisor, you have a fiduciary, legal, and moral responsibility to be scrupulously honest and always do what is best for your client, even if it costs you in the short term. Client retention is critical. It is possible for clients to work with you for twenty or thirty years, and then have their adult children continue with you after their parents pass away. That kind of long-term relationship can only develop when you put the needs of your client first.

When I was recruiting, I interviewed a woman with an impressive background. She aced her interviews and had a terrific resume. When I did a background check, I was astounded to learn she'd been convicted of a serious crime. Some people are incredibly slick and can lie without blinking an eye. Prospects know and fear this. Everyone's heard stories of unscrupulous investment firms or advisors who lost clients' life savings.

The only way to earn trust in your community is to take the long view of success. Always consider where your client will be in ten years. Will the investments you suggest today serve them in the long run? Are you creating a portfolio that matches their goals and risk tolerance, or are you just going through the motions to secure another client?

Barrier 4: Lack of Self-Confidence and Worthiness

A firm belief in yourself is essential to success in this field. Many new advisors struggle with self-esteem. Can you see yourself as the leader of a multi-million dollar business? Do you feel worthy of an abundant income, knowing you worked hard and earned it ethically? When I train a new advisor in my firm, I sit with them on client presentations and debrief each one to highlight what went well and where they can make improvements. The first time a new advisor brings in a large account, he gets excited. I'd hear things like, "Oh man, that client just moved a million dollars to us!"

While I love to celebrate wins, I always remind my advisors they should *expect* that prospects will do business with us if the advisors follow our sales process. It is essential to shift their mindset from celebrating a new client to expecting to gain a new client. Anytime a prospect does not join our agency, it's time to carefully examine what went wrong. When you have a specific preparation and sales process and follow it every time, you can anticipate a high closing rate and will believe you are worthy of it.

Confidence comes from competence. I employ an extremely detailed training process that builds the trainee's confidence over time. That tool gives me confidence in the abilities of my team, and each team member becomes confident in himself as well. One of the critical elements of our sales process is preparation. I prepare exhaustively for each appointment and teach my team to do so as well. When you are well-trained and prepared, there is no reason to be nervous or worried about getting new clients.

However, life does not automatically become rosy when an advisor begins to succeed and earns a healthy income. My son Brian, an associate advisor in my firm, started his work life as an automobile technician for Mercedes Benz. He was highly skilled at his job and made about sixty thousand dollars each year. Now, he's worked with me for six years and is earning over three hundred thousand dollars annually. I'm very proud of him and of how hard he's worked. However, he lost friends as his income increased. Former coworkers and buddies could not understand why he needed to work such long hours. Others were jealous of his income and improved lifestyle and tried to derail it.

When you change your income and lifestyle, it is likely you will need to change some of your relationships. It is essential to surround yourself with people supportive of your success and of the time required to earn it. Some of your current friends may do a great job of this. Others will fall away. Are you willing to let go of relationships that do not support you and become very selective about the new people you bring into the inner circle of your life?

Barrier 5: Lack of Personal Results

To successfully lead a multi-advisor firm, you need a track record of strong skills in sales and client retention. You will need to be the master-copy for your future advisors. If you struggle to close sales, attract prospects, or retain the majority of your clients, you are not ready to lead a multi-advisor firm.

When you recruit, you want potential associate advisors to be excited to learn from you. No one wants to hitch their wagon to a broken star. If your results are not yet where they should be, invest time in honing your skills before opening an independent agency. You can still pursue this goal but consider waiting until you increase your personal results first.

The Bottom Line

In the final analysis, who you are and what you do when no one is looking is just as important as your industry knowledge or sales skills. I've made lots of mistakes in my career and bad decisions in my life, but hopefully, the right choices outweigh the bad. No one is perfect, nor is perfection required to reach your goals. If you are willing to work hard, be ethical and honest, put your clients first, and do the personal growth work required to generate self-confidence and inspire trust, you can succeed in this industry.

M. Scott Moore

CHAPTER 20

SUCCESSION, VESTING, AND LEGACY PLANNING

This chapter briefly addresses succession planning and vesting. It may seem odd to cover this topic in a book written to introduce you to the idea of building your multi-advisor firm. However, you know by now that I am a firm believer in having a long-term plan and a clear, concise mental picture (CCMP) of your future, which is why this chapter will give you valuable food for thought.

Most of you aren't in a position to implement this material immediately. You'll need to conduct a careful assessment of your business with your CPA and attorney, as well as your business coach, before you take action on succession planning. However, I want to plant some seeds and share how I handled this question with my team of advisors.

I've always promised Chris and Brian that a portion of the company would be theirs someday. Chris came to me in 2015 to tell me he was considering moving to New Orleans and creating his own firm. It was only then that I realized I'd been so busy building the business I had neglected to take any action on my promise. Chris had been with me from the beginning, doing a great job as an advisor, and I did not want to lose him over something I forgot to do.

I took immediate action and contacted my attorney and a business valuation specialist. I also had discussions with Mark, the non-family advisor, and Carla, my wife and co-owner in the business. In about ninety days, we had a meeting where my CPA and attorney presented a succession plan, the valuation of the company, and a four-year graduated vesting schedule.

There are several options for this type of plan. I decided to gift the advisors with shares of the company over four years in thanks for all of the work they'd done to help me build the business. You may decide to sell discounted shares to your associate advisors. The four-year vesting schedule ensures they will all stay with the firm as we continue to grow and develop. At the end of the four years (2020), I will be of an age where I may desire to reduce my workload and do more consulting.

Our plan operates like this: The business is co-owned by Carla and me. Once the succession plan started, the three advisors were gifted with shares, so that at the end of the four-year vesting period, sons Chris and Brian would each own 20% of the firm, Mark 8%, and Carla and I will maintain 52% of the shares. At the end of every year, each of them receives a dividend based upon their current percentage of stock ownership.

After vesting, they may leave the firm if they wish but must give the business the first right of refusal to buy back their shares over a ten-year period. We also added life insurance policies to cover the value of their shares, so that in the event of their death, their family members will surrender their shares, but receive compensation of an equal amount of cash from the life insurance policies. These are commonly referred to as Buy/Sell Agreements.

This last portion of the plan was a bit delicate. My attorney advised me that in the event of a divorce of any of my advisors, if

I did not put protections in place correctly, an ex-wife could end up with half of her husband's equity in the business and become an unplanned business partner. Everyone, including their spouses, had to sign agreements to ensure these protections were correctly executed and would hold up in court.

Use Expert Advice

I am grateful for the guidance of my attorney, CPA, and tax specialist in creating this plan. There are personal tax implications with a plan such as this which require careful consideration. As you begin to create your succession plan, turn to experts who are familiar with state laws, the tax code, and effective succession and vesting plans.

It's More Than Money

During this process, Mark asked me a bold question. During our meeting, he expressed his appreciation for the opportunity to work in the firm and learn a valuable new career in his fifties. He was grateful for his vesting opportunity as well and felt very comfortable with his percentage of ownership.

However, he had a significant concern. He asked, "Scott, what would happen if you were to die? Chris and Brian are great guys—solid advisors—but I don't believe they have the age or life experience to effectively manage the day-to-day operations. I don't believe I could work as well with either of them as my boss."

Honestly, I had not considered this angle at all. Mark had a point. There is a difference between being a successful advisor and leading a multi-million dollar business. At the time, neither Chris or Brian had experience managing people or daily operations.

After much discussion between all of us, we came up with a solution everyone supports. Should I die, my shares will go directly to Carla. She, Chris, and Brian will compose the board of directors of the firm. Mark will be named the president and be responsible for day-to-day operations. The board will meet with Mark every quarter and give direction to the overall business strategy to guide daily operations.

Fortunately, everyone saw the wisdom of this plan. Mark is an excellent leader and mentor. Chris and Brian have known him for many years from our church, and he's earned their respect many times over. They are content to maintain their majority ownership and work under Mark's leadership until he is ready to exit the company. By then, one or both of them will be prepared to assume the administration of operations. Mark is happy to use his leadership and management expertise. Carla trusts Mark and feels comfortable with his leadership. I am relieved that should something unexpected happen to me there is a plan in place to guide the business steadily through the transition. Because Chris and Brian continue to grow, either one or both could now run the firm if needed.

With the succession plan in place, I noticed a positive change in the work environment. The associate advisors now had certainty about their path to ownership. Their motivation increased because they received a dividend on company profits each year. Staff members treated the associate advisors with more respect because they were now co-owners. Chris and Brian could now enjoy the freedom to travel, possibly purchase a vacation home, and find contentment in remaining in Georgia as part of the firm.

Creating this succession plan gave us all peace of mind, security, and enhanced loyalty toward each other. It was absolutely a worthwhile endeavor.

When to Begin Your Succession Plan

This timeline will vary for each of you. However, as a rule of thumb, I recommend you create a succession plan once your first associate advisor has been in place for five years. That will be enough time to ensure that he or she is working effectively and worthy of vesting. You may also have other associates-in-training at that time. Work with your attorney to design a vesting plan that ensures each associate maintains an extended period of outstanding service before they begin the vesting process. Again, I recommend at least five years, regardless of family affiliation.

Remember to approach your succession plan slowly, carefully, and with the support of trusted experts. Resist the temptation to say things like, "You are doing a great job. In a few years, you'll be an owner of this place." That kind of offhand comment may seem motivational but can lead to disappointments and anger if your succession looks different when you develop it. You can mention future vesting opportunities but give no firm details until you have the plan in place.

As financial advisors, we know too well that death or injury can occur unexpectedly. By creating a plan, you and your team will enjoy peace of mind and income protection. Clients will appreciate knowing that your firm will be stable no matter what happens to you. Succession planning is a win-win all around.

CHAPTER 21

WISDOM FROM THE TRENCHES

Back when I worked as a broker, I rarely had time for long-range planning or reflection. I was that rat on the wheel in a corporate cage, just hoping my next appointment would show. Sometimes I was relieved if they didn't so that I could have a break. I've learned that being the leader of my own firm requires more reflection and observation. In this chapter, I'll share a few subtle strategies I've developed over the past eleven years in my independent agency, in the hope they will help you build your success.

A Consistent Focus on Trust

Everything my firm does is designed to build trust and relationships with our clients. To that end, the behavior of all our staff members must contribute to that trust building relationship instead of detracting from it.

For example, my clients don't like voicemail or automated answering systems. In our office, staff are trained to answer all calls by the third ring. Three different staff members hear the rings for incoming calls. If the receptionist does not pick up by the second ring, the office manager or case support specialist know they are to answer. If for some reason they cannot, and the phone rings a third time, one of the advisors will answer. We always want people to know we are available to them.

I learned this lesson the hard way. Due to a snafu with my office phone provider, one day the office lost phone service. We had no idea until some newer clients showed up at the office. They were worried because they had recently moved their investments to us and soon after could not reach us by phone. Other clients were concerned too. It was a mess. Now we have systems in place to immediately notify clients if we encounter a similar issue.

Our office is open five days each week during traditional business hours. Once or twice a year, we need the entire staff to help set up for an event, so we close the office for an hour or two. We ensure that we alert clients beforehand via an email blast and place a nicely formatted and typed note on the door. It explains the situation, affirms that we will be continually checking messages, and notes our return time. In that way, we demonstrate that we care and want to be available consistently.

All my staff and advisors are trained to remember that many of our clients are seniors and expect a personal touch and a high level of customer care. We aim to make everyone feel like a part of the family. At times, an elderly client may become confused or frustrated. Recently a retired gentleman came to the office and started yelling about something. Our receptionist handled things beautifully. She did not argue with the irate gentleman, she apologized, got him a cup of coffee, and set him up to see the next available advisor. While this is a rare occurrence if you are taking care of your clients properly, things do still occur when the client may have a memory loss or other health challenge.

We also focus on establishing "procedural trust." When you employ an organized and structured approach, it is easy for anyone to note your professionalism. I have a process and form for every critical function in the office. Prospects and clients notice that we are following checklists and do things consistently. This level of organization creates trust in both our procedures and in us. When people know we are on top of all the details in our interactions with them, they trust that we will manage all the aspects of their financial transactions well too. Spend time documenting and streamlining your processes. It will pay tremendous dividends going forward.

Your Staff Represents You

As you are hiring and training your office staff, select people with excellent people skills as well as the technical skills required for their positions. I once had an administrative staff person who was outstanding with the tasks of her job. However, she'd had a long history in a fast-paced corporate environment and valued speed over relationship building. Her interactions with people were too abrupt at times.

Once a very wealthy prospect referred his son to our firm. I worked for nineteen months on this prospect—a very high net worth individual. One day his son called the office and inquired about our ideal customers. His concern was that our website focused on retirees and he was only in his forties. My staff member quickly told him that our focus was only on retirees and near-term retirees. In her mind, she was efficient and helpful. The prospect was very frustrated when his son told him what had happened. I'd been trying for over a year to build a relationship with him.

His son later called me, very upset. He felt disrespected and would not consider doing business with us, even after I apologized and told him the staff member was relatively new with our firm and that I would give her additional training. That quick and unintentional comment by a staff member potentially cost us a multi-million dollar account and offended a long-term prospect who made the referral.

Teach your administrative staff to always be gracious and

welcoming. I constantly remind my team that the office staff sets the tone for the entire business and that their primary job is to be nice, even if it takes a few minutes away from their other tasks. They are never to answer questions that should be addressed by advisors. It's not appropriate or legal for a receptionist or administrative staff member to comment on investments, the market, or anything related to an individual's portfolio.

We also continually offer clients and prospects choices, but with boundaries. For example, when we set appointments, instead of asking, "When would you like to meet again?" we will say, "Would you like to come in next week on Tuesday or Wednesday?" Once people select a day, the follow-up question is, "Would morning or afternoon be better for you?"

When everyone in your office consistently offers two choices for each decision, people feel you respect their time and will usually choose one of the options. However, the decision will be easier for them to make if you limit the options you offer. If you ask an open-ended question, all the possibilities make coming to a decision more difficult and stressful. That type of question gets people thinking about all the things they have to do in the next couple of weeks, and they may decide they just can't fit in another meeting. You could quickly lose a good prospect that way. Just like trained trial attorneys know never to ask a witness a question that will elicit an unexpected answer, you need to do the same.

In our offices, we match the dress code to community standards. Our primary office in Gainesville is in a smaller city with relaxed standards, similar to one of our satellite offices. The men in these offices wear slacks, a dress shirt, but not a tie and jacket unless they are leaving the office to speak with a group. The women wear professional clothing. Our other satellite office is located in a more formal community, so the men usually wear ties in that office. On casual Fridays, and at most client appreciation events, people wear nice slacks and a shirt with our logo. In that way, we always appear trustworthy and professional. No one wants to hand their life savings over to an office full of people in blue jeans and flip-flops.

Cultivating Long-Term Client Relationships

If you are in this business for the right reason, to help people, they can be your clients for ten, twenty, thirty or more years. Some will refer their relatives and children to you if you build the right relationships. It is crucial that you pay just as much attention to the spouse as the person in a couple who manages the finances. Generally, with seniors, the husband leads investment conversations. Many advisors mistakenly focus primarily on the husband in their interactions.

However, if you think long-term, you will remember that men generally pass away before women. In our industry, 52% of the time, widows will move money away from their current advisor after their spouse dies. After a father dies, children will often step in to help their mother, and to make things easier they suggest moving funds to the financial firm they use. Are you willing to lose 52% of your senior clients?

To prevent this client loss, I spend as much time building a relationship with the non-active prospect as the active one. I make sure to use their name every three to five minutes, direct the conversation between both members of the couple, and ensure all their opinions, needs, and questions are heard equally. Each husband or wife will have different desires such as security versus growth, and different comfort levels. As you conduct your prospect discovery sessions and annual reviews, check in with both husbands and wives to ensure everyone feels respected and is in full agreement with the current plan.

Building these stable relationships with both members of a couple can be extremely helpful as people age. If you are concerned about the diminishing capacity of one of the partners, it is very likely that their partner has similar concerns. I've had many occasions where a wife will call me privately and let me know that her husband is struggling with memory or cognition. If you have a relationship of trust with both partners, those conversations will occur more readily, and you can suggest some steps to protect their assets. One key point to note here, as I have mentioned before, is to ALWAYS transcribe any of the conversations you have with prospects or clients, no matter how small or insignificant they may be.

It's also important to minimize staff turnover. If your clients see a new receptionist every few months, they will wonder if you have instability in your leadership or your business. On the other hand, I once heard a speaker say that you must eliminate any cancer amongst your staff. He was referring to anyone with a poor attitude, an inability to conform to the values we espouse, or who is unkind to clients. If re-training such employees does not result in improvement, you must remove them from the organization.

For these reasons, I hire very slowly and check references thoroughly. I also ask people I trust for referrals of people with high client-service skills and a great work ethic. We are careful in our orientation and training as well, so that new employees have the support needed to work effectively. No one wants to do a lousy job or be unhappy in their work. When you hire wisely, train thoroughly, and then provide consistent supervision to help everyone be successful, this creates a positive and productive environment for all. There is no substitute for investing time in your hiring and staff supervision.

My current receptionist does an exceptional job, and everyone who visits our office enjoys her. She has a big heart and an innate ability to work well with older people. When she had her second child, she worried she would have to get another job to pay for the additional daycare costs. Because so many of my clients give me positive comments about how much they love her, I decided to provide her with a significant increase in salary so she could stay. She did not ask me for this raise, but I decided it was a worthwhile investment to keep clients happy and ensure the stability of our office staff.

It is also important to have an extremely efficient office manager who can decrease your tasks and handle almost any type of prospect, client or vendor interaction. I am fortunate to have a wonderful office manager who treats the company resources like her own, being very careful not to overspend on items. Unfortunately, in 2017, her husband became very sick and passed away about twelve months later. I told her to take all the time she needed away from work (with pay), and to let me know when she was ready to come back. All the members of our firm kicked in to help her. Both my wife Carla, and Mark's wife Liz (both of who used to be office managers for me years ago), filled in for her while she was off, to cover her tasks. Even though the two above examples were not of family-related employees, everyone in the firm feels like a part of an extended family, which only helps you succeed in the long run.

Invest Your Time Wisely

I used to rush around from appointment to appointment. My long days were jam-packed with speaking engagements, travel, and meetings. My viewpoint was that the faster I worked, the more money I would make. Many advisors share this belief, especially if they are working in a captive environment.

Rushing did not serve me well once I opened Moore's Wealth

Management. I learned that the more time I invested in planning, staff supervision, and relationship building, the better my quality of life and my results. I still worked extremely hard. I just built time into my schedule for these leadership duties.

Our standard practice is to set appointments two hours apart for all advisors. This schedule works well for us. With flexibility built into your schedule, you never need to rush a client or prospect encounter. Appointments generally stay on time, so people are not frustrated by a long wait when they come to the office. If an advisor has a few moments between appointments, he has time to record his notes, return calls, or respond to emails. This practice also helps the administrative staff have a more harmonious workday. We all work hard. We just work steadily.

Remember the duck on the water from chapter 7? We want visitors to our office to sense a well-organized and calm environment. We never forget that people are entrusting us with their money. Even when things are stressful behind the scenes, we strive to ensure our public image is serene.

CHAPTER 22

IN THE FINAL ANALYSIS

Now that you have reached the end of this book, just as we assess a prospect's portfolio, assets, risk tolerance, and financial needs, it's time to assess yourself. You'll either ensure that you have the proper foundation to build a multi-advisor/multi-million dollar firm right away or determine if you need more time to prepare. If that prospect comes in with one hundred thousand dollars to invest and is just a few years from retirement but needs fifty thousand dollars in annual retirement income, you know their plan is not going to work.

So, honestly assess yourself in the following areas:

1. Do you have a strong work ethic?

2. Looking long-range, what vision do you have about your income and success?

3. Are you willing to create detailed short- and long-term plans?

4. Do you have a stable family life?

5. Are you willing to live an unbalanced life during the initial years of your business?

6. How are your public speaking and communication skills?

7. Are you willing to learn new things?

8. Do you enjoy being in a leadership role?

9. How interested are you in hiring, training, and supervising others?

10. Do you have a successful sales process and the ability to close most of your prospects? Is it documented?

If you honestly answer these questions and decide that you are ready, willing, and able to follow the techniques in this book, I congratulate you. Whether you are in a captive environment or working in a one-person independent shop, my story proves that it is possible to expand and grow.

Perfection is not required, nor is a substantial savings account, or ideal health. If you wait for those things to line up perfectly, you may wait forever.

Remember the concept of Next! When you encounter a challenge or obstacle, say "Next!" and move on to finding a solution. Founding and leading an independent multi-level advisor firm is not easy. However, you will grow in confidence and leadership, win the respect of your family and community, and earn more money than you ever dreamed possible. If I can do it, you can too.

The information in this book gives you a roadmap and timeline. Customize it to suit your circumstances. I don't recommend hasty action, so do not go to work tomorrow and quit your job or hire an associate. Instead, read through this book again, making notes of the steps you'll need to follow.

I am successful because I've always been willing to admit I needed help and sought it out. I've benefited greatly from mentors, coaches, training programs, and many personal and business development books and CDs. You can find the information and support you need for every part of this journey except one: a strong work ethic. That's the only thing a coach or mentor can't teach you.

In this book, you discovered a new way of thinking about your future and the possibilities that await if you are willing to take a few calculated risks, move out of your comfort zone, and work hard. Today can be the start of your new life if you wish it to be.

I hope you decide to move ahead with your dream. Thanks to the wonderful team of staff and advisors at our firm, I am living a life I could not have even imagined when I began my career. Everything is possible with the right amount of effort, learning, planning, and the right mentors in your life.

To your success,

M. Scott Moore

ScottMooreConsulting.com

What's Next for you?

Learn More from Scott

For additional resources, the schedule of free-webinars, and to see

if you qualify for Scott's advanced trainings in Atlanta, visit www.

ScottMooreConsulting.com.

ACKNOWLEDGEMENTS

I first want to acknowledge *the Lord,* who makes all things possible and has always been an excellent guide in tough times, as well as good times. I am so blessed to have my health, my family, and the love we all share between us.

I would not be where I am today without the love and consistent support from *my dear wife Carla* and our beautiful children. You all have stood by me on every step of my journey, through the good times and the challenges. Carla, my life would be a mess without you. Kids, I thank you for being part of my life and bringing your spouses and children into our family circle. While it is fantastic to enjoy financial success, my loving family is my greatest treasure. Thank you with all of my love.

A big thank you to my very patient publisher, *Lynne Klippel.* She is one of the brightest and most talented individuals I have ever worked with on a project. Thanks, Lynne for putting up with me and for doing such an excellent job putting this book together--you are the best!

Paul Roberts changed my life when he introduced me to Gary Reed and the world of independent advisors. Paul and his wife Jo Lynn regularly opened their home to provide me lodging as I worked their area remotely. Thanks, Paul, for never giving up on me and encouraging me to step out. It took more than five years for me to take your advice and I am so grateful that I finally did. You are, and always have been, a true friend and inspiration.

To my skilled, incredible team at Moore's Wealth Management, without all of you, I would not have the lifestyle I have today and would not be able to write this book. From the bottom of my heart full of gratitude, thanks for being so coachable and loyal to me. We have all now achieved our dream- a business that takes care of others and takes care of all of us.

Bill Sowers stepped in as a friend of our family when my father died when I was seven. Even though Bill was busy with five children of his own, he took the time to help me through my youth and adolescence and kept me on the right path. Bill even helped me decide when and how to marry Carla. Bill, I know you are going through some severe health challenges, and my prayers are always with you and your wife, Betty. God Speed to both of you!

My mother had to be both mother and father to me. Mom was indeed the most optimistic person on the planet. Mom lost her soulmate too young and was left to raise three children on her own. Mom never hesitated to help others, even with our minimal family budget. Mom taught me two priceless truths: Always help others regardless of your situation, and that I could achieve anything I wanted to in life, as long as it was morally and ethically correct. Mom passed away over twenty years ago when I was thirty-five. I miss her every single day. Mom, I wish you were here today. I will always be grateful for all you did for me, and I look forward to seeing you again one day.

I can't say enough about my wonderful and supportive in-laws, *Carl and Betty Phelps*. Carl and Betty were always very supportive of whatever venture Carla and I pursued, regardless of where it took us. Thanks to both of you for believing in me and knowing I would always take care of your daughter. Carl, you left us too soon. Thank you for being like a father to me. I love and miss you and your positive attitude. Betty (Mom Phelps) I am glad you are still with us! I love you and am thankful for your inspiration of always getting the most one can out of life!

A huge thanks to *my high school buddies Tommy and Mike* who always stayed close to me and helped me through some challenging times. Tommy used to drive for seven hours to visit us and took the seven of us out to dinner when we couldn't afford to. Mike has been a true and faithful friend since before we started Kindergarten. Mike, thanks for putting up with my crazy engineer mentality, even when I counted how many times you chewed your food before you swallowed! Both of you made a profound difference in my life, especially during the challenging times--Thanks!

My business coach, Matt Miller, has taught me to use my faith in all areas of my life. Thank you, Matt, for your on-going support and belief in me. Your tremendous knowledge of the human spirit has been invaluable for me and helped me see the best in others. Your support has been instrumental in my success and a true blessing.

Gary Reed taught me more about business and managing challenges than anyone else in my life. From our first meeting, you helped me see new possibilities. This book and my success as an independent advisor all started with your vision and constant support. I can never repay you for all you have done for my family and me. You have always been generous with your time, patience, expertise, and wisdom. You are my brother from another mother, and I will forever treasure our relationship.

Finally, *John Trotter* has been my best friend and mentor for more than thirty-five years. I would never have been able to become an independent advisor without his belief in me and his economic assistance. You are my silent partner, mentor, counselor, friend, and brother. Even though you had a heavy load with your own business and family concerns, you always had time to listen and help me. Even today, your continued help and guidance makes a significant impact on my life. This book would not have been possible without you. Thank you for being an answer to prayer.

M. Scott Moore

ABOUT THE AUTHOR

For nearly thirty years, M. Scott Moore has gained experience in the financial services industry, consistently winning awards for high production and outstanding client service. As the founder and CEO of Moore's Wealth Management, Scott used the principles laid out in this book to create an independent wealth management firm with three locations, more than 600 clients, and approximately three hundred million dollars in total client assets, both fixed and actively managed. Scott is a dynamic speaker and is often invited to give presentations within his industry. Whether he is speaking to a room with 100 or 1,000 people, Scott shares his story and expertise with humor and generosity.

In 2018, Scott founded Scott Moore Consulting, an agency dedicated to training, mentoring, and advising other financial service professionals to model his success.

Before Scott found his passion for helping people protect and preserve their lifetime savings, he began his career as an engineer in the computer industry utilizing his degree in electronics from Phillips Business College in Mississippi. After nine years in the computer industry, and reaching the position of Sales Support Vice President, Scott transitioned to the financial industry where he received several top honors in his field including being honored as a distinguished "Advisor of the Year." Scott and his firm continue to win accolades for outstanding work and client loyalty.

Scott and Carla, his wife of thirty-eight years, have five adult children, ranging in age from twenty-five to thirty-seven, and nine wonderful grandchildren. In his spare time, Scott enjoys spending time with his family, traveling the country with Carla in their RV, restoring classic cars, and attending events for automotive enthusiasts.